INSTANT GOURMET

CEIL DYER

Acknowledgment

My sincere thanks to Susan Martin; without her help I could not have completed this book. Also thanks to Marjorie Sullivan and Barbara Martin for their assistance in recipe testing.

Thanks also to Paul Clyne of Southern Seasons Gourmet Food Shop in Chapel Hill, North Carolina for his helpful information on cheeses, caviar and other deli foods.

Library of Congress Cataloging-in-Publication Data

Dyer, Ceil.
  Instant gourmet.

  Includes index.
    1. Cookery. 2. Convenience foods. I. Title.
TX652.D95   1987   641.5'55   87-8584
ISBN 0-89586-546-7

Published by HPBooks, a division of HPBooks, Inc.
ISBN 0-89586-546-7
Library of Congress Catalog Card Number 87-8584
©1987 Ceil Dyer
Printed in U.S.A.
First Printing

Another Best-Selling Volume from HPBooks

Publisher: Rick Bailey; Executive Editor: Randy Summerlin
Editorial Director: Elaine R. Woodard
Editor: Jeanette P. Egan; Art Director: Don Burton
Book Design: Leslie Sinclair
Managing Editor: Cindy J. Coatsworth
Typography: Beverly Fine, Phyllis Hopkins
Director of Manufacturing: Anthony B. Narducci

Photography & Food Styling by Burke/Triolo

Some accessories for photography were from Tesoro/Mark Krasne, Los Angeles

CEIL DYER

Ceil Dyer began her career as a food publicist for wine and food companies both here and in Europe. Later she wrote a syndicated newspaper column, "The Instant Gourmet," the first of its kind to combine quick cooking with gourmet-type food. Her book *Wok Cooking* was another sensational first; in this best seller, she was the first to use a wok for both Occidental as well as Oriental recipes. Now, away from the frantic pace of New York City, she lives in a quiet resort area on the east coast, where she spends most of her time developing new and exciting recipes. She especially likes creating those recipes that make use of supermarket and deli prepared ingredients yet still have the taste of home prepared. Ceil adds her own personal touches to make the foods special.

A prolific writer, Ceil has authored more than 30 cookbooks including bestseller *Wok Cookery, More Wok Cookery, Chicken Cookery* and *Slim Wok Cookery,* published by HPBooks.

CONTENTS

INTRODUCTION
RECIPES FOR
GREAT FOOD & EASY LIVING

Between dining out and commercially prepared, so called convenience heat-and-eat-food, there is a very satisfactory and nutritious middle ground to enjoyable dining at home.

Though certainly great home cooking (so-called *haute cuisine*) can be a worthy avocation, it takes time, and except for rare occasions, these days very few of us have either the leisure or the inclination to spend hours in the kitchen. Now, however, there is an alternative to elaborate, time consuming methods of preparing meals, and it has little to do with bland, tasteless, over-priced, frozen, all-in-one package entrees. It is nothing more than the simple science and art of putting together great tasting and very individualized menus from freshly cooked dishes, precooked and cured meats, great cheeses, prepared salads and fine breads you can now find at gourmet-type takeout food shops, ethnic restaurants, delicatessens and the ever expanding array of prepared foods now available at many of today's forward thinking supermarkets. Its rules are simple and its skills are few. It's only a matter of knowing and doing.

First, dismiss the idea that all great cuisines are based on slowly cooked foods from your own kitchen. It's simply not true, as anyone who knows the preparation time for an elegant Italian antipasto or a great Swedish smorgasbord will enthusiastically testify.

Second, forget the old-fashioned American blue plate notion that every meal except breakfast must consist of meat, potatoes, vegetables, a salad and dessert. There's a world of delicious menus that are easier and quicker to prepare.

Next, expand your knowledge of what's available in your own area. In addition to gourmet-type takeout food shops, a growing number of fine French restaurants, when asked, will sell you their finest entrees, as will many equally great Italian, Near Eastern, Oriental and other ethnic cafes. Such foods need only be briefly reheated, reseasoned to your taste and garnished before serving. A tossed green salad dressed only with oil, vinegar, salt and pepper plus great bread is all that is needed to round out the menu. Dessert can be as simple as fresh fruit and fine cheese followed, if you like, by freshly brewed coffee plus an assortment of bakery fresh cookies.

Another great menu could start with an elegant cold soup (made in your own blender or processor in a matter of minutes) then go on to freshly made tortellini (cheese or meat-stuffed pasta) purchased from a cheese and pasta shop briefly cooked and dressed with either store-bought or home-prepared pesto sauce. What could be easier, yet more delicious than food such as this? For non-dieters you can add a dessert of super-rich commercially prepared gourmet-style chocolate-covered ice cream bars, sticks removed, coarsely chopped and served in your finest crystal dessert bowls. Top each serving with one or two tablespoons of Kahlua or other coffee liqueur.

This is not just a book on how to cook but one that will show you what commercially prepared foods to buy, how to take them home and transform them into very personalized meals. You will find no recipe here that takes more than its fair share of your short cooking time and none that are difficult to prepare. Both the recipes for home-cooked and store-bought dishes that you bring home and "add to" are presented with many of the quick cooking ideas I have gathered from great cooks and professional chefs from all over the globe.

The cooking methods are simple and the dishes you will create will delight a generation that is short on time but too knowledgeable and sophisticated to settle for trite and dull fare.

In short, this is a book that wants you to hurry out of the kitchen, then relax and enjoy a leisurely meal that is both delectable and nourishing.

Why Takeout Food?

These days I'm more concerned than ever before about good nutrition and, at the same time, more knowledgeable about what is and what is not so-called gourmet food. Nonetheless, like so many people, I have less and less time to prepare it in my own kitchen. That is why I have turned to already prepared takeout food. With it I save hours of shopping and cooking—precious hours I can spend in enjoying great meals with my family and friends.

With takeout food you can quickly assemble a delicious yet healthful meal when dining alone, or you can put together a party menu almost without effort. It's right for "today's type of people." It's a time and effort saver. With it you can prepare an infinite variety of totally different recipes from simple to elaborate for meals that

are interesting, quick and delicious. It's a new method of preparing many different foods.

For example, try Smoked Turkey with Pineapple, a simply fabulous dish that takes less than 10 minutes to prepare. End with freshly made coffee and any one of the quick-to-make desserts you'll find in our dessert chapter. Easy? Of course!

Or serve Poached Salmon Steaks with Salsa as the main course for an festive luncheon party. You need only add a deli prepared salad and crusty Italian-style bread for a complete menu.

Party giving comes easy with prepared, takeout foods. Just assemble a tray of imported and domestic cheeses, a platter of crisp fresh vegetables and a third platter of cold meats and serve them with an assortment of great breads. You can then relax and enjoy what you've prepared along with your guests.

Takeout food inspires you to prepare an infinite variety of different, elegant desserts, from sensational Summertime Trifle to festive yet simple Plums with Triple Creme.

Because all are assembled from readily available ingredients, such as commercially prepared ice cream; basic cakes, such as poundcake and angel food; bottled sauces and liqueurs; all are easy and effortless, yet each one is not only simple but satisfying to make and to eat.

I know you will enjoy the recipes I have assembled here and I have tried to use only those ingredients you will now find available at today's new supermarkets or gourmet-type takeout food shops. It's no fun to read an interesting recipe or try to assemble the makings of a great party when you can't find all the necessary component parts to prepare it.

Instant Gourmet Shopping

"First catch your hare"—that well-known phrase was found at the beginning of a recipe for jugged hare in an early English cookbook. Fortunately, the business of shopping for dinner no longer involves anything quite so strenuous. However, deciding what to have, buying the ingredients, then going home to face a session of cooking is often more than enough for today's kind of cook, one who has just spent a full day at work. For many years the only alternatives were to either eat out at a fine restaurant—too expensive for the average budget—or to settle for second-rate fare. But today we have a third option—really great gourmet-type takeout food. All you need to know is what, where and how to buy it. However, this is not as much work as it is fun, and can be an adventure, a new way of shopping and thinking about food.

When compiling this book, the question I was asked most often referred to nutrition, for example, "Is it as healthful as home prepared food?" It depends on what you buy as well as where you buy it. Because more and more people have less and less time to spend in the kitchen more truly great, as well as nutritious prepared food is now available. In other words, supply is beginning to keep up with demand.

When you combine deli prepared foods with raw or crisp-cooked vegetables, fine cheeses and fresh fruits plus good breads, your diet will be nutritionally sound. Here is a list of the best of the best we have found available in today's market.

BEEF

Corned beef: Brisket of beef, it is cured in brine, flavored with such things as garlic, cloves, peppercorns and other herbs for a week or longer. It is then cooked in water flavored with various herbs and seasonings until tender.

Pastrami: This delicious meat is either flanken or brisket of beef cured in a non-liquid mixture of sugar and seasonings such as crushed peppercorns, chopped garlic and coriander seeds. It is then refrigerated for one to two weeks, then dried and smoked for several hours. Finally it is steamed over water or cooked in water until fork tender.

Roast beef: The best from your deli is prepared from top round, not the entire round of beef. It is quick-roasted in commercial ovens at extremely high heat (much higher than can be obtained in the average home oven). The result is very rare to medium rare meat, however, it is best to ask to see it before it is cut. Select very rare center slices if you plan on reheating it before serving. Medium rare is usually perfect to serve cold in a sandwich or on a buffet platter. Refuse to buy end pieces; they are more often than not over-cooked, dry and tasteless. Most good delis will have a second, uncut roast beef ready and waiting to be cut.

Spiced & herbed beefs: Braised top round of beef seasoned with spices and herbs. Because of the way this meat is cooked, it will be moist and delicious. It's great for sandwich making or a cold cut platter.

HAM

The number of different hams you'll find at the deli can be confusing, everything from pressed ham to prosciutto.

Baked Virginia ham: These elegant hams are hand-rubbed with a special dry cure, smoked for days over a cool hickory fire, then aged for several months. The result is a lovely mahogany-colored ham with a rich flavor. After

should always be cut into paper-thin slices.

Boiled ham: Slightly salty flavor, mellow and mild taste. This ham is pressed into a loaf shape without additional seasonings. Use for sandwiches or serve as part of a cold meat platter.

Country hams: These Southern specialties are made in small batches throughout many parts of the South. Opinion varies as to which state produces the best. They are salty and strong in flavor, yet truly delicious. You can purchase a whole ham or buy it by the slice. Many Southerners will tell you it's the only ham to serve with your breakfast eggs, and it definitely must be accompanied by freshly made biscuits hot from the oven.

Deli baked ham: Top quality aged and boned whole hams. These hams are dry cured and/or aged before baking. Have it sliced thin for sandwiches or buffet party serving; use double thick slices when preparing hot dishes.

Ham loaf: Made with chopped lean and fat ham that is pressed with juices into a loaf shape. Whole peppercorns and other seasonings are often added. The taste is pleasant but mild. Ham loaf is a good choice for lunch box sandwiches.

Prosciutto: This classic Italian-style ham tastes totally different from any other ham you can buy; it is rich, dense and elegant. Like baked Virginia ham, it should also be cut into thin slices. It can be served as a first course wrapped around fresh melon wedges or ripe figs, cut into thin slivers and added to hot sauces, and, of course, it is traditionally part of an Italian antipasto platter.

Westphalian & Black Forest hams: These delicately flavored German-style hams are cured and smoked then aged. Although less salty and dry than Italian-style prosciutto, they can nonetheless be used the same way.

SAUSAGE

In every country where pork is produced there is sausage, and each has its own method of preparation. For an instant gourmet party or get-together, serve a variety of different sausages. Arrange the sausage on a large wooden cutting board and let your guests carve for themselves. Add deli potato salad and serve with a selection of crusty breads, a crock of sweet butter, two or more types of mustard and a variety of pickles. Here are some of our favorite sausage selections are:

Abruzzi: Cured and air-dried pork sausage with spices. A good choice for an antipasto platter, or for hors d'oeuvres.

American salami: Mixed beef and pork, seasoned with garlic and numerous other spices. Fully cooked or cured and dried or smoked.

Blutwurst: A highly seasoned, fully-cooked German-style sausage.

Brunschweiger: This sausage may be purchased either totally cooked or smoked. It's a combination of pork and beef liver, flavorful but lightly seasoned.

Capocollo: A spicy-hot cured and air-dried sausage made with pork and seasoned with red peppers.

Italian salami: A mixture of chopped beef and pork, seasoned with red wine or grape juice, garlic and spices.

Liverwurst: Smooth-textured sausage made with pork liver, ground with spices, cooked and/or smoked. The flavor is mild, the texture smooth and spreadable. Great on light rye or sourdough bread or use as the base for a double-quick pâté.

Mortadella: A smooth, subtly seasoned bologna made from finely chopped pork and beef that is both smoked and dried.

Pepperoni: An Italian-style dry sausage of beef and pork seasoned with garlic, as well as both black and red pepper.

Sopperssata: A pungent, coarsely ground pork sausage, seasoned with herbs and studded with whole peppercorns.

TURKEY

You may not remember, but only a few short years ago the only turkey available at the deli was chopped and formed white and dark meat pressed into a loaf or roll. Now you'll find everything from that same roll to turkey hot dogs, bologna and ham, as well as flavorful breast of turkey, oven roasted, smoked or barbecued, as well as plain turkey that has been boiled or steam cooked. As to flavor, it depends very much on the individual processor and the recipes used; try a variety of different brands to select the one you like best.

Bologna: Cured and seasoned, blended skinless and boneless turkey meat. We can't tell the difference between this and bologna made from red meats.

Canadian-style breakfast ham: From turkey thigh meat that has been cured and spiced with traditional flavors. This turkey meat product can be quickly pan fried or grilled, heated in the microwave oven or simmered in broth.

Hot dogs and franks: A blend of light and dark turkey meat—smoked and cured. Milder than all-beef hot dogs, pleasant but not as flavorful.

Pastrami: Skinless and boneless thigh meat, smoked and cured with peppercorns. Nice and spicy, but, in our opinion, not quite up to the flavor of red meat pastrami.

Salami & "cotto" salami: Cured dark meat, about 50% less fat than red meat salami with a very similar taste.

Turkey breast meat products: Available oven roasted, smoked, barbecued and/or water cooked, with or without skin. Flavorful and elegant to serve on cold meat platters, in sandwiches or used in quickly cooked dishes.

Turkey ham: Smoked and cured, skinless and boneless thigh meat. Flavorful yet mild, somewhat like boiled ham but less salty. An excellent choice for sandwich making.

Turkey roll or loaf: Chopped and formed white and dark meat that is steamed or boiled and formed into shapes. The flavor is boringly mild but it's nutritious; it's great for lunch box sandwiches.

Whole smoked turkey: A great choice for a large buffet party—presmoked, delicious and sensational. You may have to order this special bird, but it's well worth the effort.

OTHER GREAT FULLY-COOKED POULTRY & MEAT

Rarely will you find all of the fully-cooked poultry and meats in one shop at one time. However, most are available at one or another of the following sources in your area.

Barbecued ribs: The fresh meat department at your supermarket, a restaurant featuring barbecued foods.

Greek-style rotisserie cooked lamb: Greek restaurant or your local caterer.

Roast, rotisserie broiled & barbecued chicken: Your supermarket, takeout gourmet food shop and Southern-style restaurants.

Roast duck: The deli department at your grocer, takeout gourmet food shop, a local caterer.

Peking duck: You'll find this most flavorful of all cooked duck either in the Chinatown district of a large metropolitan area or, by special order, from the best Chinese restaurant in your town.

Stuffed & baked rock cornish hens: Specialty good shops that feature takeout food or local caterer.

All of these wonderfully flavored, fully-cooked items taste best if they are purchased only a short time before you plan to serve them. They can be left at room temperature for one to two hours, then wrapped loosely in foil, sealed and reheated in a 400F (205C) oven. If you are not planning to use them immediately, they can be wrapped and sealed in foil and placed in the refrigerator up to 48 hours, brought to room temperature and reheated as above.

You'll find ways we have used each of these products throughout this book.

SMOKED FISH

The best known, most often served and best liked smoked fish from your deli is salmon. Now, however, you'll also find an assortment of other smoked fish. Flavors range from mild to hearty and fiery. They are easy to serve and make great additions to the instant gourmet's repertoire.

Imported Scotch salmon: This imported smoked salmon is only slightly salty in flavor, the texture is firm and smooth, the flavor delicate. It is usually sold presliced and ready to serve. Serving suggestion: Arrange slices slightly overlapping on a serving platter, sprinkle with small capers, surround with lemon wedges and serve with unsalted crackers or thin slices from a long, narrow French-style loaf of bread. To make a small amount go a long way, roll each slice around a sliver of dill pickle or fresh cucumber stick. Arrange on a platter and sprinkle with minced parsley or chives.

Kippered salmon: White in color with a deliciously mild, non-fishy taste. Cut this fish into thin slices from skin side. Serve as the first course of a meal or cut slices into narrow strips and serve with deli prepared potato salad and caraway rye bread.

"Nova" salmon: A little stronger in flavor than imported smoked salmon, but with the same smooth texture. Serve this salmon "New York deli-style" on bagel halves spread with cream cheese, mince the slices and stir them into scrambled eggs, or use as a surprise filling for omelets and serve with deli rye bread.

Smoked Cajun catfish: Fired with Creole seasoning, new and newsy, especially good as a substitute for classic New York-style cream cheese and lox with bagels.

Smoked trout: These small fish average about 1/2 pound each. The skin is crispy and flecked with brown. They looked terrific placed side by side on a long serving platter garnished with parsley sprigs. To serve: Pull the skin back and remove fish from bones in chunks. Serve with a small decorative bowl of sour cream and a jar of Pommeroy or Creole mustard, plus a bread basket of assorted, thinly sliced dark and light rye bread, cut into bite-size wedges.

FISH & SHELLFISH: FRESH, FROZEN & CANNED

Anchovies: In our opinion, people who tell us they don't like anchovies are often only those people who do not like the olive oil in which they are packed. Because this oil, like bottled olive oil, can become rancid if kept too long on the shelf, it is best to buy anchovies only where they are a popular item. However, even when fresh, anchovies are highly salted; to remove excess salt and oil, you can rinse them briefly under warm water and blot dry before using. We like to chop and add them to salads, omelets, scrambled eggs, or just about anything else. What's more, we found that if we did not

tell those "hold the anchovy" people what they were eating, we often received compliments on our flavorful cooking.

Canned salmon: The best, though unfortunately the most expensive, is labeled "Sockeye." We use it in much the same way as tuna. It can be drained, cut into thick slices and topped with bottled bernaise or curry sauce. We also break it into chunks and add it to commercially prepared hollandaise sauce to spoon over toast.

Canned tuna: We try always to have on hand one or more small cans of tuna, either packed in olive oil or water. When dining alone and too tired to cook anything—we simply open the can, drain off the liquid and pile it onto the center of our dinner plate, top it with a bit of mayonnaise, sometimes mixed with a few capers, then surround it with whatever crisp-cooked or raw vegetables we have on hand. Or, we use it to make a simple salad, or stir it in into canned soup. The best is solid pack tuna either in water or olive oil. Don't buy tuna in oil unless it is a popular item at your particular market; despite assurances to the contrary, the oil can become rancid if it sits overlong on the shelf.

Fresh & frozen fish: I'm sure you know, all fish must be cooked quickly to retain its moisture and flavor. The only acceptable fish for the instant gourmet are already boned, skinned and cut into fillets. Then, for those of us who do not have time to stop off at our fish market on the way home from work to buy them fresh and cook them the same day they are purchased, there are the relatively new individually frozen fish fillets. They can be stored in the freezer of your refrigerator for several weeks, do not have to be thawed before preparing and cook in a matter of minutes.

Fresh shrimp: When buying fresh shrimp, we prefer to buy the jumbo-size variety in the shell. Because they take much more time to prepare than to cook, we serve them in the shell and let everyone peel their own.

Herring, in wine sauce, in sour cream or in vinaigrette dressing: If you'd like to transform deli cold cuts and potato salad into a Swedish smorgasbord, add two or more types of herring to the meal. Include Emmentaler, Swiss and Norwegian Jarlsberg cheeses; Swedish-style flat breads; light and dark rye spread lightly with unsalted butter; hot mustards; crisp pickles; a can or so of Norwegian brisling sardines and imported beers.

Imitation crab blend: This blend of crab and whitefish makes a delicious substitute for crab-meat. Though milder in flavor than "the real thing," it is inexpensive by comparison and can be used in the same way. With few exceptions we prefer the fresh blend available at the fish market over those from the freezer section of our supermarket. We have used it, with sensational results, in our Seafood Stir-Fry with Tomatoes (see page 77).

Sardines: There are so many delicious ways to serve sardines they belong on everyone's emergency shelf. They are one of the best, most thrifty, most nutritional buys on the market today. One little inexpensive can will make a sandwich or a salad. They are as great to take along for an alfresco-type picnic as they are to serve as an appetizer along with predinner drinks. For a sandwich filling or dip, mix two cans brisling sardines with one 3-ounce package of cream cheese; add Dijon-style mustard and lemon juice to taste.

CAVIAR—THE ULTIMATE LUXURY

Fish eggs, or roe, can be obtained from any number of fish, but the most luxurious and, incidentally, most expensive comes from sturgeon, and, by law, is the only caviar that does not require any other labeling. Less expensive caviar must be identified as to the type of fish, for example, red salmon, white fish, or lump fish. In the nineteenth century, American caviar was part of the free lunch offered in many saloons. No more—because of its rarity, caviar from sturgeons now costs $150 to $300 for a 12-ounce tin—definitely a luxury item.

There are three principal kinds of sturgeon caviar. Beluga caviar is shiny black and large. Osetra has smaller eggs and tends to be slightly brownish in color. Severuga eggs are the smallest. Beluga is the rarest and the most expensive caviar you can buy in today's market and, of course, it has the greatest cache. But because Osetra is considered to have more character and flavor, it is rapidly gaining in popularity.

Also rapidly gaining in favor is American caviar. This newly revived industry which flourished in the early part of this century, but was fished out and became extinct for roughly 60 years, is definitely "back in business." Much less expensive, American caviar outsells Russian caviar in America six to one, and many experts believe its just as flavorful as the Russian type.

The classic way to serve caviar is on toast strips or thin slices of black bread first spread with sweet butter. Most enthusiasts insist that champagne should be the only accompaniment. Though this is an expensive combination, it's marvelous. For the instant gourmet who would like to give the ultimate party of the year, it just may be the answer, and, if you pause to consider the work and expense involved in putting together a more extensive menu, you may discover that extravagance costs less than you think.

How much to serve: we like to plan on one bottle of champagne and two ounces of caviar for every two or three guests. Obviously some people will eat and drink more while others will keep to much less. Being generous, however, has its bonus—you can celebrate with leftovers later in the week.

FRESH MEAT SECTION OF YOUR SUPERMARKET

Here's where you'll find some of the best cooked meat, chicken and turkey; tender, juicy pink roast sirloin of beef and top round of beef, beef brisket, meat loaf more like a country pâté than the traditional homemade version, and kabobs of juicy beef skewered between green bell pepper and onion chunks. There are barbecued chicken —the entire bird, and plump tender "ready to heat-and-eat" turkeys, including juices that can be quickly made into a delectable gravy.

The meat products are fully cooked, wrapped and sealed airtight. They are fresh, not frozen, and can be quickly heated by placing the package in a microwave oven for 3 to 4 minutes or submerging the package in a large pan of boiling water for about 10 minutes. They are great served right from the package or can be used when making double-quick, truly instant gourmet recipes.

Barbecued chicken need only be unwrapped and placed in a preheated 375F (190C) oven until hot. Fully cooked and oven ready turkey will take you only a fraction of the time it takes to prepare an uncooked bird and is delicious.

FRESH MARINATED MEATS

These fresh marinated meats began to appear at the service meat counter at our supermarket only a few short months ago—and do we love them. All the prework has been done for us and all we need do is broil or grill them, which only takes from 8 to 10 minutes. Any of these meats can be purchased one or two days ahead, after which they can be frozen for several weeks. Though the extra marinade can only be kept in your refrigerator two to three days, because it has already tenderized and flavored the meat, its use is not absolutely essential. Though there are many different varieties at our own supermarket, the ones we have tried and liked best are veal chops with mustard, rosemary garlic lamb chops and marinaded London broil.

DELI SALADS

Salads that come from the deli are more varied, more flavorful and better than ever before. You can serve them straight from the carton or give them a luxurious boost with a few special additions. To add flare and your own special touch to any deli salad, consider the following suggestions:

Carrot salad: Add drained pineapple tidbits or crushed pineapple. Stir in strips of green pepper or celery. Add chopped dried apricots or other minced dried fruits. Stir in small fresh green grapes.

Chicken salad: Add small calamata olives or chopped Niçoise-type olives; fold in fresh tiny white grapes; stir in a bit of Dijon-style mustard; add peeled, cored and chopped crisp apple. Fold in slivered almonds or chopped walnuts. Serve salad over fresh peeled and pitted peach halves or mound on small plates and surround with slices of avocado, sprinkle surface with minced chives or onions.

Health salad: Add cold cooked rice. Mellow dressing with mayonnaise.

Macaroni salad: Add pitted, chopped ripe green olives; chopped cheese, such as fontina or Swiss or grated Parmesan cheese; a sprinkling of minced chives or green onion.

Old fashioned potato salad: Add peeled, cored, and chopped apple; thinly sliced or chopped celery; chopped fresh green or red bell pepper; chopped sour gerkins or drained capers. This salad looks great when served on large thick slices of sun-ripened tomato and sprinkled with paprika.

Pasta salad: Stir in fresh mung bean sprouts or crisp shredded lettuce. Add fresh tomato strips. Stir in a bit of bottled pesto sauce or chopped fresh basil leaves. Add thinly sliced Genoa salami or other cold cuts from the deli. Stir in slivers of baked Virginia ham or other cold cuts.

Shrimp or seafood salad: Add additional coarsely chopped shrimp, crabmeat, lobster or imitation lobster meat; stir in a bit of Dijon-type mustard and chopped pickles or pickle relish. Top salad with whole shrimp or large pieces of other seafood. Serve on slices of fresh pineapple; garnish with additional seafood.

Three bean salad: Add freshly cooked, chopped new potatoes or freshly cooked small pasta shapes; chopped celery or green pepper strips. Mellow dressing by stirring in a bit of mayonnaise.

Serve any deli salad in tomato shells or avocado halves. Stir sour cream into any deli salad made with a mayonnaise-type dressing. Serve salads in crisp lettuce leafs, surround with tomato wedges and top with minced chives.

FROM THE SHELF: GREAT FOODS FOR NON-COOKING

Though the following items are certainly not all of the good things you'll find at your grocer, we've singled them out for the following reasons: almost all are work free, all are multi-purpose (they can be used in a number of different ways), and each has passed our final test—most people find them delicious.

Bernaise & curry sauces: Rich and delicious, these bottled sauces are never-fail good. Both may be used as a hot sauce for such diverse entrees as eggs benedict or curried shrimp. Serve over fresh or canned asparagus, spoon from the jar onto hot cooked vegetables just before serving, or use as a topping for baked potatoes.

Canned broth and consommes: Though it's only our opinion, we prefer full strength chicken and beef broths that are ready to use (not condensed). Occasionally we take time to give them that "homemade" taste—it's easy and quick. Place two cans of broth in a saucepan, add any or all of the following: about 1/4 cup minced green onions or 1 small finely chopped Vidalia onion, a small scraped and thinly sliced carrot, a few trimmed and chopped mushroom stems (if available), and 1 or 2 tablespoons dry sherry. We let it simmer over low heat for about 30 minutes, after which we strain it through a fine sieve, discarding all solids. Either use it right away or pour it into a storage bowl and keep it in the refrigerator for up to three days, or place it in the freezer, where it can remain fresh and flavorful up to one month. For the beef broth, we add about 1/4 pound freshly ground lean top round of beef to the other vegetables, strain and store it in the refrigerator until all fat has risen to the surface and can be spooned off before the broth is used.

Canned Italian caponata & mushroom salad: Drain and serve either one of these canned Italian specialties as appetizers with cocktail rye bread rounds, sliced French-style baguettes, or chunks of Italian-style bread. Or add them to crisp salad, or drain, mix with cream cheese or butter and use as a sandwich filling.

Canned soups: The best in our opinion are those that are of the "heat-and-serve" variety, rather than those that are condensed. Exceptions: a new, creamy natural soup from Campbell's that requires the addition of milk instead of water before heating. When preparing it, we often add a chopped fresh vegetable corresponding to the type of vegetable used in the soup. On the list of our other favorites are the Italian-style soups made by Progresso, to which we often add cooked noodles or rice to transform them into a hearty main course.

Canned vegetables: Though some vegetables cannot be successfully canned, others seem to hold up well during this process. Best in our opinion are kernel corn, beets and lima beans. These are almost always part of our emergency shelf provisions, we use them most often in salads and casserole dishes, or simply sautéed in butter as an accompaniment for a main course entree.

Chutney: Though chutney is considered an essential accompaniment to most curry dishes, it also has so many other uses. We find it an essential addition to our emergency shelf. In this country the most popular type is labeled Major Grey's, a generic term for a sweet-and-sour mixture of mangoes flavored with ginger and garlic. However, you'll now find a number of other chutneys at your grocers made with a base of peaches, apples or other fruit. Any one of them can be used to enhance just about any type of food.

Serve chutney with cold deli meats, add a few tablespoons to deli chicken, shrimp or tuna salad, use as a spread for cheese sandwiches, or serve as an accompaniment to takeout fried chicken.

Commercially prepared pasta sauces: Some are good, some excellent, and a few are exceptionally flavorful. However, here again it's a matter of taste; your choices may differ from mine. For the most part, we prefer those without meat. If you want to give these sauces a truly homemade flavor, start by sautéing a few raw vegetables, such as chopped onions and green peppers in butter until slightly softened. Pour in the sauce and stir until heated, then add one to two tablespoons of grated Parmesan cheese. Even if you're going to serve cheese to sprinkle over each serving, the melted cheese gives a additional depth of flavor to the sauce.

Garlic paste & bottled pure garlic juice: To our way of thinking, either of these products tastes more like fresh garlic than the small jars of garlic powder you'll find on the spice shelf at your supermarket.

Imported English pickled onions & small water packed cocktail onions: Large pickled onions are especially good when served with beer, but they also make a superb accompaniment to cold meat platters as well as to salads and hearty sandwiches. The small white onions make an easy yet elegant hot vegetable, either heated in butter, cream sauce, cheese sauce or commercially prepared curry sauce. They also can be used in place of fresh onions for quick-to-prepare beef stew. Or use them as part of an antipasto platter or as an accompaniment to hearty sandwiches such as corned beef on rye.

Kumquats in heavy syrup: The perfect dessert for an Oriental-style meal. Drain and spear each with a colorful cocktail pick, serve with almond cookies or fortune cookies—or drain and chop these exotic members of the orange family and serve along with a bit of their syrup over ice cream or sherbet. Chop and mix them with softened cream cheese, spread between thin slices of date nut bread—a sandwich to impress the bridge lunch crowd.

Lemon juice from concentrate: We like to keep this bottled juice in the refrigerator as a wonderfully easy substitute for fresh lemon juice when we don't have fresh lemons on hand.

Marinated artichokes: Drain and serve as an appetizer, chop and add them to salads, or use them as an accompaniment to the main course entree.

Marinated vegetables: Though there are many others equally good, our favorites are pickled okra, dilly beans and three-bean salad. Both the pickled okra and beans can be drained and served "as is" for appetizers or as an accompaniment to sandwiches or salads. The three-bean salad is good simply drained and spooned onto crisp lettuce. To make an exceptional salad, drain, toss with thinly sliced fresh celery, green or red bell pepper strips and canned whole-kernel corn.

Oriental sesame oil: This seasoned oil adds flavor to both Oriental as well as Occidental-style food. Sprinkle sparingly over either home prepared or takeout Oriental dishes—add a few drops to canned or homemade clear soups—add to vinaigrette dressing for oriental-style salads or use in quickly made glazes when reheating fully cooked takeout chicken, duck or turkey from the deli. You'll find a number of different recipes using this oil throughout this book.

Oriental sweet & sour sauce & plum sauce: Serve either or both of these sauces with Oriental-style takeout or home prepared dishes, or try them with very Occidental takeout fried chicken, deli beef, or sliced turkey breast. Use them, as we have done, in an all-in-one Dinner on a Plate (page 100) to marinate jumbo shrimp.

Pesto sauce: There are several different brands of this flavorful mix of basil leaves, pureed to a paste with olive oil and Parmesan cheese. Though you can of course make this sauce for yourself, the usual recipe requires from 2 to 3 cups of fresh basil leaves—hard to come by unless you grow your own. It has many uses: Stir it into tomato sauce for pasta, mix it with cream cheese and spread on crackers, stir it into scrambled eggs or into just about any sauce when you want an extra dimension of flavor.

Pickled baby corn: A wonderful addition to an Oriental-style stir-fry, or an Occidental salad plate. These tiny ears of corns can also be drained and served with predinner drinks.

Salsas: These hotter than hot Mexican-style condiments can be served as a dip with takeout Mexican food. It's great on nachos served with beer or non-alcoholic drinks, and, of course, they can be added to home prepared Mexican sauces and stews.

Sesame paste: This Near Eastern product made from sesame seeds has much the same consistency as peanut butter and can be used in the same way. The flavor, however, is much more subtle and though it makes a splendid nut butter and jelly sandwich, it can also be used in many other ways: as a base for elegant salad dressings and dips, as the thickening agent for stir-fried dishes, or as a subtle seasoning for both Oriental and Occidental-style sauces, soups and stews.

Soy sauce: Today you'll find a confusing array of different soy sauces on the shelves of even a small supermarket. They vary from an American-made low salt version to imported brands that are dark and heavy in flavor. For the occasional Oriental cook, the best buy is an all-purpose, medium light soy sauce that has been aged before bottling.

Sun-dried tomatoes: The intense flavor of these tomatoes can make a superb addition to just about any cold or hot entree—for a no-work luncheon platter, serve them with a wedge of Brie or Camembert accompanied by crusty slices of French or Italian-style bread. Drained and cut into slivers, they can be added to any salad, either yours or one from the deli, or they can be tossed into freshly cooked pasta along with plenty of butter and Parmesan cheese.

Tahine paste: This smooth, creamy thick mixture looks like a pale version of peanut butter and can be used in the same way, but it is also the base for a superb Near Eastern-style sauce or salad dressing and it makes a splendid dip for raw vegetables.

Tomato paste & paprika paste in tubes: Both of these products are simply great to have on hand, especially so if you want to use them in small quantities. Unused portions can be refrigerated in the tube for several months.

Water-packed artichoke bottoms: They make wonderful appetizers, either stuffed with cream cheese and topped with chives, or, if you're in an expansive mood, red salmon caviar. They can be simply cut into cubes as a go-with for predinner drinks, added to stir-fry dishes, served in place of a hot vegetable with your entree, or used in casseroles.

Water-packed sliced fresh ginger: These crunchy non-sweet slices of fresh ginger root save you the time and trouble of peeling and slicing ginger root from the produce department, yet they are as crisp and flavorful. For stir-fry dishes, of course, but also for crisp, freshly made salads—use them in place of sliced celery or radishes.

HERBS & SPICES

For many years my kitchen shelves were stocked with a large variety of different herbs and spices, sometimes as many as 20 or more. However, because many were purchased for one recipe only then left unused for such a long time, they lost their pungency before we used them again. This, I have discovered, was a waste of good money that could have been used in many other delicious ways. So, as my stock diminished, I did not replace them, substituting instead these two all-purpose basic mixtures that I could use in their place: mixed French herbs and mixed Italian herbs. With few exceptions, they're all we need for average, everyday cooking.

Mixed French herbs can vary slightly but are usually a mix of thyme, basil, savory and fennel. A bit of lavender is added to the special blend of Herbs de Provence to give them the fragrance of that area.

Italian seasonings usually consist of marjoram, thyme, rosemary, savory, sage, oregano and basil.

These herb mixtures can be purchased at many gourmet-type food shops in bulk and by weight. Buy only the amount you plan on using within two to three months.

FRESH PASTA & FRESH OR FROZEN GOURMET-STYLE PASTA SAUCES

As more and more small cheese and pasta shops have begun to appear in almost every large city, it becomes easier than ever to pick up the makings for a quick yet hearty supper on our way home from work. Fresh pasta is pasta that is not totally dried out, though it can be and sometimes is frozen. It is at its best when it has been prepared no more than two to three weeks before it is cooked and served. The same holds true of specially made, gourmet-type pasta sauces. Pasta is usually made with special seasonings such as basil or other herbs to give them extra flavor. And because they are fresh, they are more tender and take less time to cook than the packaged and dried varieties. As to the sauces, they are usually more highly seasoned than bottled or canned sauces. As to whether they are better, more flavorful and more to your taste than bottled or canned sauces, it depends very much on where, how and who has prepared them. We can only recommend that you try one or two from different shops then make your own decisions.

ORIENTAL NOODLES

The big news about pasta is that not only can you now find fresh pasta in most supermarkets, but there is an increasing number of Oriental pastas on their shelves, including what we are now labeling Oriental vermicelli. Why hasn't someone told me about this pasta before? It does not have to be cooked. Just place it in large bowl, add boiling water to cover, let stand until softened, then drain and serve. I love it, you'll love it, not only for its ease of preparation but also for good flavor. And you don't have to limit its use to Oriental-style food; you can use it for everything from Italian sauces to California-style pasta salads.

THE OIL OF THE OLIVE

Like fine wine, olive oil gets its flavor from the soil and climate as well as the type of fruit from which it is pressed. But unlike fine wine which must be aged to reach its peak of perfection, olive oil is at its best when freshly pressed.

Buy olive oil where it is a popular item: a gourmet food shop, an Italian grocery or one of our new super-supermarkets. If left on the grocer's shelf for only a short time (two to three months), it will darken and become rancid in the unopened bottle.

Buy olive oil in small quantities. Once opened, store it in the refrigerator—never at room temperature, under neon lights or in direct sunlight. Though it will thicken and look cloudy when cold, it will be clear and thin as soon as it reaches room temperature—10 to 15 minutes.

The pick of the olive oil crop, called **extra virgin,** comes from the very first pressing. It is less acid than virgin olive oil, with a mild and mellow taste. **Virgin olive oil** is also made exclusively from the fruit, though it may be from a second pressing. **Pure olive oil** has been refined to remove impurities, then blended with virgin oil to bring up its flavor. The acid content is about 3.3 percent.

We prefer to use extra virgin oil for salads. Pure oil is good for cooking but for extra flavor we usually blend it with an equal amount of butter. To pick a favorite, buy a small bottle of several different brands. Some will be nuttier than others, some denser and some will taste more strongly of olives.

OTHER GREAT OILS

Almond, hazelnut & walnut oils: Sweet and delicate, these oils are splendid to use for vinaigrette dressing. They tend to lose flavor and become rancid quickly, so buy in small quantities and use soon after opening.

California avocado oil: Seldom does a totally new product appear on the market—certainly not one as flavorful and versatile as this. The light buttery flavor of this oil is best experienced in cooking. When sautéing at low temperature nutty flavor is imparted to the foods. At mid-range cooking temperature the buttery avocado notes are brought forth and when combined with a delicate touch of herbs and spices, entirely new dishes can be created. At very high temperatures this oil has no equal. Very high sustained heating without burning or smoking of the oil allows for exceptional stir-fry dishes as well as deep-fried foods.

This oil is a marked departure from other fruit oils. It is processed slowly by mechanical means, without chemicals, which captures the light effervescent flavor of the fruit. It has the highest smoking point of all fruit oils and can be used for everything from sautéing to deep-frying. Julia Child called it "a perfect substitute for butter." It can be used in baking to replace

half of the amount of melted butter, in sautéing where the rich avocado flavor comes out, in marinades for beef, chicken or fresh fish, or in preparing vinaigrette or other salad dressings.

Herb flavored oils: Olive or grapeseed oils that have been flavored with herbs or spices. We prefer tarragon to all others, but other herbs and seasonings such as basil, bay leaf, garlic and peppercorn are often used.

Sesame seed oil: This is a seasoning oil, used sparingly. Add to Oriental-style dishes, sprinkle very lightly over takeout Oriental entrees, add to vinaigrette dressings for Oriental-style salads, or add to softened sweet butter and use as a sandwich spread.

MUSTARD

Possibly the oldest and certainly the most used condiment in the world today, it is said that the Chinese were the first to cultivate the mustard plant, grind the seeds and mix it with liquid to serve with seafood and meat. Today it is used in such diverse cuisines as French, German, English and Oriental. No wonder—it adds an intriguing flavor to just about any food from hot dogs and hamburgers to soufflés, salads, soups and sandwiches. Just a few short years ago here in America there were only two types of mustard: mild and sweet or mildly hot. Now, you can find a mustard to suit every taste, every type food you plan to prepare. Even the color ranges from pale yellow to green to dark brown!

Creole mustards: There are several different brands. These mustards are only medium hot with a sweet aftertaste. They are great with baked ham or other cold cuts from the deli.

Dijon-style mustards: Made with mustard seeds that are hulled and combined with vinegar or white wine and spices. The flavor is just medium hot. Its smooth texture and subtle flavoring makes it the most versatile for either cooking or using as a condiment.

Grainy mustards: Made with whole or coarsely chopped mustards seeds. Possibly the most famous is Pommeroy mustard, originally made in France but now prepared here in the United States. The flavor is fiery hot. We like to use it as a spread for deli roast beef.

Hot mustards: These are usually of English or German descent. Great with any cooked sausage. This is the type of mustard most often served with Chinese food.

Peppercorn & herb mustards: Made with red or green peppercorns, or such herbs as tarragon, basil and dill, these mustards give a tang to prepared cream sauces or a vinaigrette dressing.

Sweet mustards: Mild and tangy, but only moderately hot, this type of mustard is still America's favorite for hot dogs. It is also great on hamburger patties as well as deli ham and turkey.

Wine mustards: Mustards flavored with sherry, red wine or even champagne. Elegant and expensive, but well worth the price.

GREAT BREADS FROM THE BAKERY, DELICATESSEN & FREEZER

For many people bread is more than just bread, it is a statement, a way of life. Many Americans still refuse to eat any but the bread of their childhood—often the soft, tasteless, packaged white loaves. For others no bread is worth eating unless it's prepared from stone ground whole wheat and includes a liberal sprinkling of wheat germ—while for Francophiles, a freshly baked crusty-style loaf is the only acceptable bread. But for the instant gourmet bread can be an adventure in eating and anything goes if it's flavorful and will fit into our general menu. Serve sourdough bread from San Francisco with a California-style salad, Syrian flat bread for a Near Eastern-style sandwich, French-style bread for breakfast lavishly spread with goat cheese and served with fresh fruit, or piping hot biscuits with Southern-style takeout fried chicken and ribs. For these reasons, our only recommendations are to buy them fresh and keep them fresh by placing them well wrapped in the freezer compartment of your refrigerator where they will stay fresh for many weeks at a time. Because they thaw quickly, take them out of the cold no more than 30 minutes before using.

Belgian-style waffles: These rich golden-brown waffles are a full 1-inch high, crispy on the outside and fluffy within. They contain no preservatives or food coloring. Serve them with butter and honey or maple syrup for breakfast, spread with cream cheese and jelly for a mid-morning snack, or top them with ice cream and hot chocolate sauce for dessert.

Boboli: A fat, round loaf, thicker than pizza dough but flatter than bread. This is a prebaked cheese-topped focaccia-like bread, that is firm, close-grained and satisfyingly chewy. It can be used as an accompaniment to any meal, or used as a base for pizza. For breakfast it can be topped with cream cheese and fresh fruit. Serve it for lunch as it comes from the oven, or cut it into thin wedges and serve with dip as an appetizer.

Focaccia: Another flat, round, chewy loaf that is a direct descendant of the earliest kind of bread made. Its name comes from the Latin word focus, which means "hearth." Long before ovens were invented, bread was made by flattening the dough then baking it on a stone or terra cotta slab on the hearth. Imported from Italy in airtight, colorful foil packages, this bread may be kept at room temperature for a few days or placed in the freezer until ready to use. It needs only brief heating. It is delicious as a snack, with a meal or as the base for any number of different pizza toppings. For a mid-morning snack, brush it with sweet butter and sprinkle evenly with brown sugar, place in a 350F (175C) oven and bake for 5 minutes. To serve with a luncheon salad, brush generously with mild virgin olive oil and sprinkle with chopped onions before heating. As an appetizer, use olive oil and coarse salt or with a meal, replace the salt with crumbled or minced fresh or dried herbs.

FROM THE FREEZER

Frozen French sauce bases: These highly concentrated beef, chicken and fish stock reductions can transform the short-order cook into a fine French chef. Frozen stock bases are concentrated stock made from fresh bones, fresh vegetables and herbs that are simmered for hours until only the pure, delicious essence remains. These bases contain no artificial preservatives, no artificial flavoring or coloring, and no monosodium glutamate (MSG). They are sugar and fat free. No salt or starch is added. They can be used straight from the freezer or thawed before using. If you do not need to use the entire container at once, you may chop off the desired amount and refreeze the rest.

You can substitute this stock in any recipe calling for homemade or canned stock, commercially powdered stock or boullion cubes. They are the basic ingredient used when preparing almost all classic French sauces. You need only add such additional ingredients as cream, butter and seasonings. Though certainly you can make this stock concentrate in your own kitchen, as you may know if you have ever done so, it takes much attention and literally hours to prepare. Its very existence in gourmet-type takeout food shops and now, finally, at supermarkets is good news for anyone who has ever spent hours preparing fine French food. For a fact, there's virtually no end to its uses in making and preparing great soups, sauces and stews. You'll find a number of recipes using this product throughout the following chapters.

FRESH PÂTÉS & TERRINES

Though originally considered two totally different types of food—terrines were meat mixtures baked in earthenware casseroles while pâtés were originally baked in pastry—they now mean the same thing: finely ground meats and vegetables blended with such flavorful ingredients as truffles and mushrooms, liqueurs, brandy or sherry. Though you can, of course, make your own pâtés—if you can find all the necessary ingredients and if you have at least a day to spend in the kitchen. Unless you're extremely experienced and knowledgeable about the making, the kind you buy will not only cost you less money but are better than the home prepared varieties. You'll now find two or more freshly made pâtés at your supermarket, but, at this writing, you'll still find the largest variety of pâtés only at a takeout gourmet-type food shop.

When buying pâtés it's best to ask for one or two samplings before you buy, not only to ascertain if they are indeed fresh, but also to find one that satisfies your own particular taste.

Serve pâtés either cut into cubes as a go-with for predinner drinks or serve them, as the French do, cut into thin slices and served on crisp lettuce leaves as a first course for a party meal. Accompany with a few sour cornishon pickles and crisp crackers or thin slices from a long, narrow, crusty loaf of French bread.

CANNED PÂTÉS

When you don't have the time or the money to buy fresh pâtés (they are expensive), buy the canned varieties; they can be exceptionally good and are wonderful to have on hand whenever you want to add a festive touch to the meal.

Pâtés are made with a base of duck liver, chicken liver, finely ground sausage, salmon or other fish, or vegetables. Serve pâtés not only when you want to impress, but when you want to enjoy them yourself. Easy, elegant and delicious, they can change a simple luncheon or dinner into a memorable meal.

OLIVES

And garnish with olives—how many recipes end with this sentence? Literally dozens, I'm sure. Olives and pickles are more than a garnish; they're a wonderfully flavorful foods that can enhance everything from frozen creamed chicken to pasta dishes. What's more, each type has a distinctive flavor of its own.

Here are some of our favorites:

Calabrese: A mild bronzy green olive. Slivered and tossed with freshly made pasta, fresh tomato slivers, minced parsley and freshly grated Parmesan cheese, they make a sensational entree.

Calamata: Considered to be the most flavorful of all olives; this purple-black almond shaped olive is a must for Greek-style salads. They make a great addition to Caesar salads and can bring any "Chef's salad" from ordinary to special.

Greek ripe olives: This pungent, brine-cured olive has an assertive flavor. They are often sold in bulk in many delicatessens. Chop and add to sandwich spreads, scatter over an antipasto platter, or add to deli prepared chicken, tuna or seafood salads.

Niçoise: This small French olive is brine-cured then packaged in oil, sometimes with herbs. They are a must for Niçoise salads.

Olivata: This flavorful mixture is made from minced ripe olives, extra virgin olive oil and herbs. It has many uses. We especially like to add it to cream cheese or mayonnaise to use as a sandwich spread, stir it into commercially made sauce for pasta, or into sour cream to serve as a dip.

Ripe alfonso olives: Large and delicious, yet mild; we like to cut them into slivers to add to creamed chicken or creamed chipped beef. Served whole they make an elegant appetizer.

Royal or victoria olives: These large Greek olives are cured in oil; the flavor is wonderful yet mild. We like to serve them as appetizers with cheese or add them to a platter of cold meats.

Sicilian: These small cracked green olives are cured in salt brine. Sliced with red pepper and oregano, their pungent flavor makes them a perfect foil for mild cheeses.

Stuffed green olives: At one time these olives were painstakingly stuffed with strips of pimento, now however, though still flavorful, the stuffing is commercially made.

PICKLES

Like olives, pickles make a great garnish, but each type has its place with or in certain foods.

Cornishon: These tiny, very sour pickles are traditionally served with pâté de foie gras, but they also enhance any pâté.

Dill pickles: The best you can buy are sold in large jars in their own brine, either at the deli department of your supermarket or at deli take-out restaurants. More than any other pickle, these should be crisp. Great with pastrami and corned beef sandwiches, salads, or chopped into takeout cole slaw or potato salad.

Gerkins: These extra-crisp, sweet and yet sour pickles make a good accompaniment to deli meats, especially hams.

Pickle relish: Here again the brand you buy is most important. These relishes can range from rather sweet to almost sour, but the best in our opinion is in the middle range; just slightly sweet, just slightly sour. It belongs on hot dogs, but it also can make a flavorful low calorie spread for sandwiches when mixed with creamy-style cottage cheese. Or stir a little into any warm sauce such as cream sauce or tomato sauce for pasta for added flavor.

Sliced sweet pickles: When buying these pickles, select a top quality brand with crisp and crunchy slices that are indeed sweet yet tart. A very American pickle, they belong in almost any sandwich, but especially in hamburgers.

Sweet mixed pickles: Drain, chop and add to home prepared or takeout salads, especially good with chicken or tuna salad.

CAPERS

These tiny deep green beads of flavor are an especially good buy for anyone who relies heavily on frozen dishes and deli prepared food, often adding just the right touch of picquant flavor. Imported primarily from France, Italy and Spain, these small jars seem expensive but they can be refrigerated indefinitely without fear of spoilage and as even a teaspoonful or so can make a tremendous impact, they are well worth the price.

But what are capers? They're the flower buds of the caper bush, a thorny plant that thrives wild in hot, dry Mediterranean climates. Though some connoisseurs claim the best tasting capers are the small, French nonpareilles ("without equal"), we have found the larger, less expensive Italian variety equally delicious. Both are prepared in much the same way: after harvesting they are dried in the open air, then pickled in a cask of salted white vinegar or dry-cured in coarse salt. To remove some of the saltiness, you can rinse them before using.

Here are a few suggestions for their use:

• Add 1 to 2 teaspoons to commercially prepared tuna or chicken salad.

• Roll thin slices of deli roast beef. Arrange in a single layer on one long platter or on individual salad plates; sprinkle with capers and a little of the caper juice.

• Add capers to sour cream and serve with crisp fish sticks, or over lightly breaded, frozen, cooked fish fillets.

• Add to tomato sauce for pasta.

• Cook frozen spinach following directions, drain and stir in a few capers.

• Melt butter over low heat, stir in a few capers and serve over steamed vegetables.

• Cook spaghetti or other pasta, drain, return to hot pot, stir in butter and capers.

• Heat 1/4 cup avocado or olive oil in a small heavy skillet; stir in 2 or 3 tablespoons drained small capers and toss with small noodles.

• Stir capers into softened butter, season with lemon juice. Use as a spread for turkey or roast beef sandwiches.

FRESH PRODUCE

As any nutritionist worth her vitamins, calories and minerals will tell you, a well rounded and healthful diet must include fresh vegetables and fruit. But what to do when you seldom have time to buy and prepare them? Eating out is seldom the solution. Though restaurant vegetables can look and taste great, more often than not, much of their nutritional value is lost by cooking and/or simply standing around waiting to be composed into a salad. Well, here are some, if not all of the answers.

Buy "salad bar" prepared vegetables but only from a market where they are a popular item and have been on display no more than one to two hours. If left standing under neon lights all day, much of the nutritional value is lost. Cauliflower, broccoli and baby carrots are your best buys—as are chopped celery and green pepper. All save considerable preparation time in your own kitchen, however, chopped iceberg lettuce, the least nutritional lettuce you can buy, and tomato wedges, often unripened and "seedy," seem to us superfluous—after all, how much time does it take to slice a tomato or prepare more healthful greenery?

These are not all of the vegetables you'll find at your market, but only those that have the best keeping quality, are easy to prepare and cook in a matter of minutes.

Belgian endive: This small, elongated lettuce with a tight fitting head requires little or no cleaning. It can be stored in the crisper bin of your refrigerator for up to one week. Cut off and discard the tough root end, cut across into slices and toss with vinaigrette or any commercially prepared dressing and serve as a salad. Or chop leaves and add them to deli prepared salad. Chop and add to stir-fry dishes; sauté briefly in butter to serve as a hot vegetable. Separate leaves, stuff the root end with cream cheese or other soft cheese and serve as an appetizer.

Cucumbers: For many years the only cucumbers available at the supermarket were heavily waxed, making the skins inedible. Now, however, you'll find the long, thin, almost seedless cucumbers, sometimes referred to as "Burpless," unwaxed and wrapped tightly in thin plastic wrap. If stored unwrapped in crisper bin of refrigerator, they will remain crisp and fresh for eight to ten days. Cut into thin slices, toss with vinaigrette or other dressing and serve as a salad. Cut crosswise into 1/4-inch slices, spread slices with cream cheese or other soft cheese and serve as an appetizer. Chop or slice and add to stir-fry dishes; cut into finger-length strips, steam briefly or sauté in butter and serve as a hot vegetable.

Mushrooms: For best keeping quality, buy loose, not packaged mushrooms, with caps that fit tightly to stems. (When caps have unfurled and show their pleated undersides, they are past their prime.) Store, unwashed, in crisper bin of refrigerator. They will stay fresh for two to three days. When ready to use, wipe clean with damp paper towels, trim off root end and serve small mushrooms whole. Remove stems from large mushrooms and reserve for other use. Fill caps with cream cheese or other soft cheese; serve as appetizers. Chop or slice mushrooms; add to stir-fry dishes. Slice and stuff into takeout hamburgers, or chop and add to deli prepared salads. Sauté briefly in butter; serve as a hot vegetable or stir into takeout main courses.

Parsley: "And garnish with sprigs of parsley." How many recipes end with this sentence? Too many, in our opinion. For best keeping quality, wash sprigs under cold running water, blot partially dry, wrap loosely in double thick paper towels and store as directed above for spinach. Chop just before using; sprinkle over hot cooked food or add to home prepared or deli salads.

Romaine lettuce: Prepared as directed above for spinach leaves, this greenery will stay fresh in the crisper bin of your refrigerator for three to four days. Cut across into shreds just before using; toss with vinaigrette or other salad dressing and serve as a first course salad or toss into deli prepared salads. Add to stir-fry dishes just before serving or sauté briefly in butter and serve as a hot vegetable.

Spinach leaves: Buy only loose, fresh, small, undamaged leaves; wash each leaf thoroughly under cold running water. Shake off excess water but do not blot dry. Roll damp leaves loosely in double thick paper towels; towels will absorb the moisture and keep the spinach fresh for several days. Use for spinach salad or a salad of mixed greens, or add to deli prepared salads or stir-fry dishes.

Zucchini & yellow squash: Do not wash, store in the crisper bin in refrigerator up to one week. Trim and slice or coarsely chop; place in a large bowl, add sufficient water to cover and drain into a colander. Add to deli prepared salads, especially carrot or "health" (raw vegetable) salad, or add to all-in-one plate entrees, or sauté briefly (about 1 minute) and serve as a vegetable.

FRUITS

Although fresh fruit, as you know, is shipped to us—"posthaste"—from all over the world and strawberries may appear in your market in the middle of winter, you'll be rewarded with better flavor and lower prices when you can buy locally grown, in-season fruit at its height of perfection.

Apples: You'll find at least one or more varieties of fresh, crisp apples at your supermarket almost every month of the year. For best keeping quality, store them in your refrigerator crisper bin until ready to use. All apples are great for eating "out of hand" any time of the day, but they also have many other uses. Peel, core and chop apples; add to takeout or home prepared stir-fry dishes; peel, cut in thin slices, remove seeds and add to takeout hamburgers or other sandwiches. Chop and add to home prepared or deli salads, or serve, French-style, with cheese wedges for dessert. Provide small paring knives and let each guest peel his or her own.

Apricots: A simply superb fruit when fully ripened; tender to the touch, sweet to the tongue and full of rich flavor—however, because they are picked too green, we seldom find them this way in our supermarkets. To bring out their best: split in half, remove stone and place cut side down on a steamer rack over simmering water only until slightly softened. Serve them cut side up topped with a little creme fraîche, triple creme or mild fresh goat cheese.

Avocados: Yes, they are a fruit and one of the most enjoyable you'll find year round at your market. Let them ripen at room temperature or in a sunny window until the skin yields readily to the touch. If they are ripe before you want to use them, store them in the crisper bin of the refrigerator where they will keep for up to one week. Peel, remove stone and cut lengthwise into wedges, top with thin slices of proscuitto or other flavorful ham and serve as an appetizer. Cut in half, remove seed, peel halves and fill with home prepared or deli salads, such as chicken, tuna or seafood. Or simply fill the cavities with a tangy vinaigrette dressing and serve as a first course for a seated dinner. Sauté slices briefly in butter or avocado oil, sprinkle with salt and serve as a hot vegetable. For dessert, serve avocados as they do in Latin America with lime juice and sprinkled with powdered sugar. Make Guacamole Salad, see recipe on page 131, or simply mash ripe avocados, mix with a bit of lemon or lime juice and serve as a spread for your breakfast toast.

Bananas: No they're not fattening, and yes they are extremely good for you, containing a considerable amount of potassium as well as other minerals and vitamins. For the instant gourmet shopper it is best to buy only a few that are fully ripened, a few that are yellow but still firm and the remaining still green. Keep them at cool room temperature and eat as they ripen. If overripe, you can refrigerate them without loss of flavor or nutrition for several days longer. This versatile fruit can be added to fruit salad for luncheon, sautéed in butter and served as a vegetable with the evening meal, or used for dessert. Try them sliced, mixed with a rich, commercially prepared chocolate sauce and topped with either sweetened whipped cream or creme fraîche, or use them to prepare Fruit Flambé (see page 148).

BERRIES: Fresh berries are at their peak of perfection during the midsummer months when they are fully ripened. To store, remove them from their cartons and transfer to a colander; remove and discard any that are overripe. Do not wash—place in a bowl lined with paper towels and store on the lower shelf of your refrigerator until ready to use; they will stay fresh for three to four days. Wash just before using.

Blueberries: Cultivated blueberries, the kind sold in supermarkets, usually come to us slightly underripened and tart. Stir them into any home prepared or deli salad or sprinkle lightly with sugar and serve for dessert.

Blackberries: The large cultivated blackberries found in today's market are somewhat seedy, but they are heavenly when stirred into sweetened whipped cream.

Raspberries: To our of way of eating, these

are the most luscious, the most glamorous of all fruits, and no other berry can match their seductive flavor. Serve them with or without a light sprinkling of sugar over top quality vanilla ice cream and sprinkle with Framboise (raspberry brandy).

Strawberries: This is another fruit that is eaten from morning to late night. Washed and blotted dry they can be served with stems attached to be dipped in sugar and eaten by hand. Stir into a commercially prepared melba sauce; fold into omelets for breakfast, brunch or supper. Use in fruit salads, add to fruit compote, or use to prepare our light and airy Berry Puff for a festive brunch menu.

Cherries: The best in the market are the large, lusciously sweet Bing cherries. Serve on the stems to be eaten by hand, or halve and pit them to serve over vanilla ice cream for a lavish dessert, especially when each serving is sprinkled lightly with cherry heering or cherry-flavored liqueur.

Kiwifruit: Look for fruit that yields easily to the touch, denoting it is ripe, or buy it as we usually find it, rock hard and unripened. At home keep it at room temperature, turning occasionally until softened. Peeled and cut crosswise into slices, it makes an attractive addition to a luncheon or dinner plate. Because the flesh is only slightly sweet and a little tart, it can be served as part of a main course but it also makes a flavorful as well as colorful addition to a fruit salad bowl or a compote of mixed fruit to be served for dessert.

MELONS: Some melons are seasonal, others like cantaloupe, are widely grown and can be found in the market throughout the year. The best way to select a ripe one is to ask the head of your produce department to pick it out for you; he will know more about selecting it than you. In general select a melon that has a rich fragrance.

Cantaloupe: Halve and eat for breakfast, fill small melons with sherbet and serve for dessert, or cut into cubes and add to a compote.

Casaba: These white-fleshed melons make an elegant first course, peeled, cut lengthwise in wedges and topped with proscuitto.

Crenshaw: When fully ripened, these melons are wonderfully fragrant and truly delicious. Peeled and seeded, cut into wedges or cubes, they need no further embellishment.

Honeydew: A great melon to cut into cubes and add to a fruit compote but they are also a wonderful breakfast fruit. Cut lengthwise into thin slices and serve sprinkled with lemon juice, place slices around a scoop of cottage cheese, or sprinkle with a little vinaigrette and serve for a very diet-minded lunch.

Persian: These melons have a breathtaking flavor and bouquet when fully ripened. They are at their best when slightly chilled and served "as is" for a dessert.

Tangerines, mandarin oranges, satsumas, & tangelos: These fruits all belong to the same citrus family and though each has a slightly different flavor they all have these pleasant attributes: a fragrant bouquet, a flavor that is more sweet than tart, and skin that is easy to peel. Select fruit that is heavy in the hand—full of juice—and serve them with or between meals, for breakfast, with luncheon dishes or as a light dessert. Stored at a cool temperature they will remain fresh up to two weeks.

Peaches: Fresh peaches are at their best when only slightly chilled; if underripe, keep at room temperature until the skin yields easily to the touch. When fully ripened, store in refrigerator for up to a week. Serve them for breakfast topped with heavy cream. For lunch, peel, halve and remove pits, place on lettuce-lined plates and top with anything from cottage cheese lightly seasoned with vinaigrette to deli prepared chicken, tuna or seafood salad. Or use them for glorious desserts such as Peach Melba or Peaches Flambe.

Pears: Supermarket pears are usually picked too green and artificially ripened. Though they never approach the tree ripened fruit, we always find a place for them on our menu. When poached or steamed until softened, we top them with heavy cream, creme fraîche or mild goat cheese. Or slice and serve them over ice cream or with cheese for dessert.

Pineapple: Now that we can obtain fresh pineapple that has been peeled, cored and packaged in airtight plastic bags, they often appear on our table. It keeps better if it is removed from the package, sliced or diced and stored in a covered bowl in the refrigerator. We serve pineapple sliced and broiled with our entrees or chopped and added to stir-frys. Include fresh pineapple in a fresh fruit compote lightly flavored with liqueur, served on or under ice cream and topped with either chocolate or raspberry sauce.

Plums: Buy fully ripened but still firm fruit. For best keeping, store them in the crisper bin of your refrigerator where they will keep up to a week. Bake or poach them in a light sugar syrup flavored with liqueur and serve for dessert. Chop and add to fruit salads, or steam and serve with home prepared or takeout entrees.

SELECTING GREAT CHEESES

Buying fine cheese can be very simple or extremely complicated. You can stay with a tried and true favorite, ask a knowledgable cheese merchant to make your selection, or buy and try a variety of different cheeses until you've built up a repertoire of those you like the best. Cheese, like any other type of food, is simply a matter of taste.

This section is designed only to assist you in finding your way through the various types of cheeses now available at your market. After each, we have listed those considered by many to be the best of the best from each type.

FRESH CHEESE

Cottage Cheese: Many years before the time of Miss Muffet and for some time after, this cheese was home prepared in the farmhouses and small cottages of rural England. Though now factory made, we Americans eat more of this type of cheese than any other. Fresh, uncured and only one step removed from milk, it is made by only draining the curd. Very moist, it is ready to eat immediately. At its best, its flavor is mild with only a light tang; quick to sour it should be chosen with only one major thought in mind—that it be fresh.

Cream Cheese: This fresh, unripened cheese is as double rich as the name implies. It is not aged, develops no rind, and is generally mild flavored with only a slight tang. The best, to our way of thinking, is made without vegetable gum or other additives. It is soft and more spreadable than the familiar foil-wrapped package variety and though generally more expensive, it is well worth the price. Though you'll now find this type of cream cheese at the deli department of many supermarkets, you are more apt to find it at health food stores or gourmet-type takeout food shops.

Farmer's Cheese: This is whole milk cottage cheese with the liquid pressed out and some cream added. Though more and more supermarkets are adding this type of cheese to their shelves, the best, in our opinion, still can be found at specialty cheese shops or gourmet takeout food shops where they can be purchased either by the slice or by the pound.

Mozzarella: Italy's other famous fresh cheese, made by a more complex method known as *pasta filata,* "spun paste." The curds are warmed then kneaded like bread dough. Originally this cheese was made with pure water buffalo milk but more often than not, the buffalo milk is now mixed with cow's milk (usually one-third buffalo milk). The flavor is much like that of a young goat- or sheep's-milk cheese. Shipped to this country packaged in its own brine, it can be stored in the refrigerator in its liquid for up to three weeks.

Here in this country Italian grocers still often make their own mozzarella from cow's milk, usually from a commercial starter. These soft, slightly chewy balls of cheese are sometimes smoked or rolled with thin slices of proscuitto. We use them as a topping for our own boboli pizza, chop and add them to salads or, because they soften into thick oozy fillings, use them for hot sandwiches or as a stuffing for chicken. The commercial mozzarellas sold in supermarkets in plastic-wrapped packages are somewhat rubbery, and though they make a stringy, fun to eat topping for pizza, the flavor is lackluster. Much preferable is the mozzarella sold by the slice or pound at the deli department of your supermarket or at specialty food shops, which is much more flavorful and tastes more like those made by Italian grocers and have the same smooth melting qualities.

Ricotta cheese: This cheese has a definite split personality; in Italy, where is was originally developed by thrifty cheese merchants, it was not considered a true cheese but a cheese-like product made from the whey given off by the production of other cheeses. Here in the United States, because the curd is used as well, it is considered a true cheese and is used frequently in Italian-style dishes such as raviolli and lasagna. But it is also a great cheese to substitute for butter or use instead of cottage cheese in the center of a salad or vegetable plate.

SOFT RIPENED CHEESE

Though many excellent soft ripened cheeses are made in many parts of the world, their excellence is still measured by cheese merchants and connoisseurs by comparing them to those made in France. Soft, satiny, buttery smooth and rich, these glorious cheeses have an interior that, when served at their peak of perfection, has a fragrant and full bouquet, and a taste that leaves a fruity, lingering tang. These cheeses get their remarkable elegance from the way in which they are made and ripened. Soon after the cheese has been separated from its whey and before it is put to cure, its surface is sprayed with a white mold, related to penicillin. The cheese is then placed in a cool, dry room for about a week during which it becomes firm and a downy white rind begins to appear on its surface. It is then transferred to a cave for about ten days. From there it is ready to send to market.

Though we would happily eat these cheeses for breakfast, lunch, dinner, or any time in between, because they are expensive, we usually save them for entertaining, confident that they will be appreciated both by those who know these types of cheeses as well as by anyone who has never before experienced their excellence. They can be served as an appetizer with crisp crackers, with salad when served as the last course of a meal, or as dessert with fresh fruit.

Brie: Poems have been written and songs sung —honest—about this most famous of all French cheeses. Brie is a mild, delicately flavored cheese with a downy rind that's edible. When cut into wedges, the creamy yellow center spills generously from the crust like honey. Its flavor is like no other cheese; somewhat like mushrooms and truffles, with an earthy taste that is nonetheless like fine cognac. To understand its fame, Brie should only be eaten at its prime, however, because this cheese comes in a large size, the average customer buys a wedge rather than a whole cheese and can therefore see whether the center is creamy and yellow throughout, glistening from top to bottom rind, or whether the center is still chalky and unripened. The finest Bries are made in the village from which they originated. Examples are Brie de Melun and Brie de Meaux.

Camembert: Camembert in France is what Cheddar cheese is here in America. It is the most popular, most often served cheese. It is also one of the least expensive, nonetheless it is prized by connoisseurs around the world who give the same attention to its selection as many more costly cheeses. This is a plump disc of a cheese, about 1-1/4 inches in diameter and 1-1/2 inches thick. It becomes flecked with gold as its reaches it prime. All French Camemberts available to the U.S. market are produced from pasteurized cow's milk and all are packed in a traditional small light wooden box invented in the late 17th Century especially for this cheese. A ripe Camembert should fill its box, be full and plump, and smell fresh. It if feels relatively hard to the touch, it is not yet ripe. If it has too much golden brown on its surface, it only has a short life left. Essential to the perfect Camembert is that it be kept whole until it is ripe. If it is cut too early, the natural ripening process is upset and the cheese may never reach perfect maturity.

Carre l'Est: You'll find this cheese wrapped in foil and sold in small 4-inch squares. Its flavor is reminiscent of a mild Brie. A delicious and reliable cheese, it is an excellent choice when served as a dessert cheese with fresh fruit.

Coulommiers: This is another soft ripened cheese from France, a cousin of Brie, made as a small, round pie. It shares Brie's subtleness and bouquet.

Fromaggio Granduca: A recently developed Italian Brie-type cheese with a delicate taste and creamy interior, and a flavor that is delicate yet rich and buttery.

Tradition de Belmont: This American-style Brie is made in Wisconsin. Though milder than the French Brie, it is an excellent alternate.

Toma di Carmagnola: A 12-ounce buttery cheese also from the Piedmont area of Italy, it has a pleasant mild, nutty flavor and is an ex-

cellent dessert cheese. We especially like it with ripe Anjou pears, crisp water biscuits and accompanied with espresso, richened with a few tablespoons of pear liqueur.

DOUBLE & TRIPLE CREME CHEESE

These soft, creamy little cheeses are as rich and luxurious as a cheese can be. Easily spreadable, their textures range from that of whipped cream to softened cream cheese, with flavors that range from delicately mild to tangy. Though both types are made from cow's milk, triple creme has a higher butterfat content making it an ideal dessert topping. These cheeses appeal to both those who love cheese as well as to many who think they do not.

For a luxurious breakfast or brunch, spread croissants with double creme cheese and serve with freshly brewed coffee or Italian cappucino. For the cocktail hour, spread crisp crackers with double or triple creme spiced with herbs or pepper. We use triple creme to replace whipped cream or we serve it along with crisp crackers as dessert, occasionally with brandy or other liqueur.

SEMI-SOFT CHEESES

Cheeses in this category could just as easily be called semi-firm because their texture can range from sufficiently soft to spread with a knife to firm enough to slice. All are soft and buttery and can range in flavor from tangy to mild, with a pleasant nuttiness. These cheeses are made by pressing the curd to eliminate most of its moisture, then they are aged for several weeks, usually rindless. A few of these cheese are coated with a layer of wax or paraffin, others are simply pressed into blocks and can be cut either into thick or thin slices. These cheeses have excellent keeping qualities. Most can be kept at cool room temperature from ten days to two weeks before they begin to dry out and harden. In the crisper bin of your refrigerator they can be kept sometimes a month or longer without becoming dry or moldy. If molding does occur, it can be scraped away, leaving the rest of the cheese edible— and if it becomes dry, these cheeses can be grated and stored in an airtight container for several months. Use the grated cheese to sprinkle over casserole dishes, into eggs for scrambling, or toss with just cooked pasta.

This group includes so many great cheeses that it is impossible to include even those generally considered the best of the best here in America. For that reason we have listed only those our small panel of experts tell us are Americans' top favorites.

Bel Paese: This is a semi-soft cheese made from pasteurized whole milk in a small town near Bologna, Italy. It has a buttery texture, a rich and mellow but delicately tart flavor. Salt content is low. It is an exceptional cooking cheese, but it's also great as a table or dessert cheese with fresh fruit. While the name itself means "beautiful country," this well-known cheese tastes "beautiful" as well.

Fontina: Made in both France and Switzerland as well many others countries including the United States. Considered the best of this group is Fontina dal D'aosta, an incredibly smooth, buttery, creamy cheese that adds richness to sauces, but also elegance to a cheese platter. Made with raw milk, this cheese gains flavor and increases in aroma as it ages. Next in popularity is Italian Fontina, sometimes called Formpal. Smooth, mild and nutty in flavor, it's an all-purpose cheese that can be served alone or used in cooking.

Harvarti cheese: An extremely appealing yet mild flavored cheese that can be served from morning to night. Serve for breakfast or mid-morning snacks, for luncheon sandwiches, as an appetizing addition to cheese and ham platters, or in cooking for any meal of the day.

Monterey Jack: This American original was first made by Spanish missionaries in Monterery, California while trying to develop a simple white cheese. They were more than successful; with our growing interest in American-made products, Monterery Jack is fast becoming as familiar to us as Swiss or Cheddar. The best of these cheeses are still made by relatively small companies in California, but they're also made in Wisconsin as well as other states. Monterey Jack is a mild, creamy cheese made from whole milk, and it is sometimes flavored with bits of hot pepper, minced salami, onions or chives. Either way, this is a great cheese to use in sandwich making, serve with Mexican-style food, grate over hot chili or melt over casserole dishes.

Provolone: Possibly the most popular of Italian cheeses. It comes in a variety of sizes and shapes and the flavor varies from mild and buttery to piquant and sometimes smoky. It's a fine cheese to add to a luncheon or light supper buffet.

Port-Salut: This mild, creamy French cheese was developed by Trappist monks in the Monastery of Port-du-Salut. We like this cheese on crusty French bread or in sandwiches such as that old favorite, a club sandwich made with baked ham and smoked turkey breast.

WASHED CHEESES

Washed rind cheeses have an assertive aroma and lusty flavor that can range from pleasantly zippy to compellingly strong. These cheeses are made like soft ripened cheeses in the first stage of their production. However, their curing time is much longer and unlike soft ripened cheeses, they are not sprayed until their final curing time in the cave and, only during their final curing period are they washed with salt water, beer or brandy in order to thicken their crust and maintain their moisture.

Brick: Sometimes referred to as the beer cheese, it comes in convenient brick logs that make it perfect for hearty sandwiches such as those made with caraway rye, spread with mustard and rare beef. It is also a good companion to German-style sausages and pumpernickel bread. The flavor is assertive but not quite as compelling as Limberger. Obviously it is at its best when served with German or other beers.

Epoisses: This century-old cheese of Burgundy is a supple flat disc with a smooth, shiny rind. Brushed with the local brandy of that region, it has a delicate flavor and aroma that becomes increasing strong as it matures.

Limburger: The strong, pungent flavor of this cheese with its overwhelming aroma that becomes increasingly sharp even after it has been packaged and placed under refrigeration, is often considered by many a cheese not to be eaten but to be avoided at all cost. When young, however, it is a truly wonderful cheese to serve with strong ale or hearty beer. It belongs with flavorful mustards and breads such a pumpernickel and dark rye. Made in Germany as well as the United States, it is a cheese for people who prefer hearty foods and strong flavors.

Liederkrantz: This is America's most popular washed cheese. Developed here by Emile Fray, a German immigrant, it has a butter smooth white interior covered with a rust colored rind. The flavor is assertive yet mellow, becoming increasingly strong as it ages. Today Borden in Ohio makes this cheese and wraps it in boxes that are dated to show its age. This cheese is removed from the shelf if not sold while still young.

Pont l'Eveque: High on the list of French cheese, the making of Pont l'Eveque dates back to the 13th Century, proceeding the making of Brie and Camembert by several hundred years, but made in much the same way. However, curing time is two to three times longer. It is a small, plump cheese with a golden rind marked by the straw in which it has sat during its six-week curing period. Its interior is soft and pale yellow, the taste carries a pronounced tang and the aroma is savory. A unique and very French cheese, its assertive flavor is satisfying rich, a cheese in a class by itself, so original it is difficult to compare with any other.

CHEVRES

No longer considered rare or exotic, chevres—cheeses made from goat's milk—are fast becoming America's luxury cheese. Whether French, Italian or American made, we've become addicted to their zesty, fresh taste. Mild, creamy chevre can be substituted for cream cheese. For a sophisticated version of a cream cheese and jelly sandwich, use crusty Italian bread, cut from the center of the loaf, spread with Montrachet and sugar-free marmalade or Major Grey's chutney. Or serve crisp unsalted crackers spread with a New York State goat cheese and crisp apple slices. For a zesty spread, whip a small amount of heavy cream into a soft, mild chevre and season with herbs, black pepper and grated lemon zest; spread on crusty French bread and serve with ripe olives. We like to combine soft, mild chevres with ricotta cheese as a filling for little, crisp, commercially prepared tart shells or add it to a white sauce and stir until smooth and creamy.

Bucheron: Fat, log shaped French chevre with a soft, light ivory rind and a snowy white, chalky interior.

Caprella: A round, flat Italian import with a rind like a Brie with a creamy, smooth interior.

Chevreese: A fresh chevre made in New Jersey. One of our favorite cheeses.

Montrachet: A soft and creamy chevre produced in the same region of France as the celebrated white wine of the same name.

Pyramide: Zesty, fresh and particularly mild with a typical goaty flavor. Pyramide becomes increasingly hard and pungent as it ages.

CHEDDAR & CHEDDAR-TYPE CHEESES

Here's another cheese that spills over into several categories, from semi-firm, mild and sliceable, to sharp, crumbly and very firm. With few exceptions, before the first World War, Cheddar was the only aged cheese made in America. For many people in those times, cheese was Cheddar and Cheddar was cheese; for some it still is. Even today it is still the most popular for everyday buying. These cheeses are made from either raw or pasteurized cow's milk. After the curd has been separated from the whey, the curds are stacked in molds and pressed to eliminate all liquid. Their flavors depend very much on the type of milk used and the length of time they are aged. These cheeses do not develop rinds—the best are wrapped in cheesecloth, then dipped in paraffin or wax that let them breathe and age slowly. The most flavorful, in our opinion, are those made from raw milk and aged for six months or longer.

Cheddars are equally good with or in soups, made into sandwiches, eaten "out of hand" for between meal snacking, or used in cooking for anything from a flavored Welsh Rarebit to an elegant soufflé. We use grated or crumbled aged Cheddar to flavor soups, fill omelets, or top casserole dishes. If you'd like to make commercially prepared frozen beef or chicken pie taste almost "like home," top the crust after it is browned with a slice of Cheddar and bake until softened. Or pour commercially prepared soup into heatproof bowls and top with a slice of Cheddar, then place them a few inches under broiler heat until the cheese has almost melted. Wow!

American varieties: Some of the best American Cheddars are made in Vermont, New York and Wisconsin. New York State Cheddars are exceptionally good if aged from 9 to 18 months. Sharp in flavor and crumbly in texture, they are great for "eating out of hand" with crisp apples or mellow pears. They are delicious in rye bread sandwiches or served with warm apple pie. Vermont Cheddars are more mellow and moist. Easily sliceable they make the best of all grilled cheese sandwiches, but they also add interesting flavor to omelets, Tomato Rarebits, or cheese sauces. Mild, mellow Wisconsin Cheddars, including Colby and Longhorn, are versatile, all-purpose cheeses. They can be sliced for sandwiches or cut into cubes for snacking, shredded and sprinkled over tacos, meaty chilies and refried beans. A good choice for turning hamburgers into cheeseburgers or hot dogs into "Coney Island Red Hots" to be served with cold beer.

Canadian Black Diamond Cheddar: So named because it is considered in that country of diamond quality and is coated in black wax. Aged from one to three years, the texture is crumbly, the flavor medium-sharp.

Cheshire: This is England's most ancient Cheddar-type cheese, known throughout history since the days of the Romans. It is creamy and rich, with a mellow tang due particularly to the natural saltiness of the milk produced in the Cheshire pasturelands, once covered by prehistoric seas. This is an excellent all-purpose cheese, great in salads and sandwiches and delightful as a dessert with crisp nuts and mellow red wine. It is also a good melting cheese to use in recipes.

English Cheddar: For the most part, it's milder than our American product. It has a clean, creamy, nutty taste—with a fine balance between not too sweet and not too acid and a mild extra "kick" that gives it personality.

Wensleydale: Another great Cheshire-like cheese made in Yorkshire, England where it originated. Wensleydale is a traditional accompaniment to a tart apple pie. A bit flaky in texture and pale in color, this cheese has a subtle flavor with elusive hints of honey and sour cream. We like to serve it as a dessert cheese with walnuts or crumbled over sliced apple rings on buttered toast.

SWISS & SWISS-TYPE CHEESES

Swiss cheese is now a generic name for any large, semi-firm cheese with holes scattered throughout its interior. First made in Switzerland in now what is termed Emmentaler, it is one of the most widely copied in the world today, or should we say, at least the holes are copied. Although some copies are excellent, none are quite like the original; made from fresh, unpasteurized, partially skimmed cow's milk, it is one of the most difficult cheeses to make, taking both knowledge and skill. It also takes time, frequently much more time than is given to other Swiss-type cheeses.

Selecting Swiss or Swiss-type cheeses depends very much on how you want to use them. We select a well-aged Emmentaler in preparing a Swiss cheese salad or when making a creamy smooth fondue, and also for cutting into finger-length sticks to serve as appetizers. For a chef's salad of mixed meats and cheese, we use a domestic type called Lorraine or Norwegian Jarlsberg which is milder than Emmentaler Swiss, yet has a little more flavor than many American brands.

BLUE VEINED CHEESES

Whether you prefer strong assertive flavors or prefer those that are mild and mellow will determine your like or dislike of these distinctive cheeses. These cheeses vary from semi-soft to semi-firm, from creamy to crumbly, and from relatively mild to decidedly strong in flavor, but it is their blue-green veining that distinguishes them from all other cheeses. Blue veined cheeses come by their veins either naturally through their aging process or by being innoculated with a strain of penicillin (totally different from antibiotic penicillin) to help start or hasten the process. Unlike soft ripened cheeses which develop from the outside in, blue cheeses ripen from the center out and, as the cheese develops, the blue-green vein spreads evenly to the outer rind. To bring blue veined cheese to its maturity it is necessary to age them in damp caves or cave-like rooms for at least three months, and because they are usually rubbed with salt, they do not often develop a rind. Fully matured, these cheeses should be decidedly flavorful but never harsh. Served at their peak of perfection, they will be creamy or firm yet never dry, the aroma strong but not unpleasant, and the blue vein should appear relatively evenly throughout the cheese from center to edge. These cheeses will keep for a relatively long period of time in the refrigerator, but keep them away from delicate food that might pick up their flavor. Usually sold in foil wrapped wedges, bring them to room temperature in their decorative wrapping until just before serving.

American Blues: These true blue American cheeses, once considered inferior to their European cousins, are now coming into their own. The best in our opinion are Maytag Blue from Ohio, Bresse Bleu from Wisconsin and Minnesota's Treasure Cave. Maytag Blue is a creamy white cheese with a distinctive, but mild flavor. Bleu is creamy and mellow yet tangy, much like the French Bleu de Bresse, and Treasure Cave is made with raw milk and aged in caves for almost four months. Because these cheeses are less expensive than those made in Europe, we happily use them when preparing salad dressings and dips and serve them with luncheon salads or hearty suppertime soups.

English Stilton: Generally acknowledged as the king of English cheeses, Stilton is one of England's most widely talked about and most praised cheese. It has a soft texture and a tantalizing flavor that is most appreciated when served as a dessert cheese with fine vintage port or Madeira.

Gorgonzola: Named for a village near Milan, this classic blue-green veined cheese has a soft, smooth, yet crumbly texture. At its best it should have a sharp but not over pungent flavor. Although most Italians serve this cheese for dessert with unsalted crackers or crusty bread, it is also frequently used in a salad dressing.

Roquefort: This aristocratic cheese is one of the world's oldest, dating back to the days of the Romans. It is made from sheep's milk and ripened in the natural limestone caves of Combalou in south central France. Though there are many other excellent blue cheeses made in other parts of France as well as many other countries of the world, Roquefort is one of the world's most memorable.

Scandinavian varieties: Danish Bleu, sometimes labeled Danablu, Finnish Bleu and Swedish Bleu all are firm, crumbly cheeses with a heavy lacing of blue veins. Though they lack the elegance of the great blues, they are reasonably priced so they can be used in cooking—to fill omelets, and turn hamburgers into cheeseburgers.

GRATING CHEESES

Though you can save money and time by buying these cheeses already grated in neat little cardboard containers, in our opinion they're hardly worth taking home. These inexpensive Parmesan-like cheeses are often not true Parmesan, but a blend of American-made Parmesan and other hard grating cheeses. Far better are the kind you'll find at the deli department of your supermarket, either freshly grated or in chunks. These cheeses quickly lose flavor once grated and are at their best when grated only a few hours before using. Because they can be kept in the freezer compartment of your refrigerator for many months without loss of flavor, they are your best buy.

Though there are a few other cheeses used for grating, when we think about this type of cheese, we think of "Parmesan."

Asiago: Originally a sheep's milk cheese from Italy, it is now made from cow's milk here in the United States.

Montasio: A cow's milk cheese from Italy, usually aged from 12 to 15 months, it is a mild flavored cheese that can be substituted for Parmesan when you're cooking for someone who prefers a light flavoring.

Parmesan: We seldom give a distinction between one or other type, it is more often than not listed simply as Parmesan. However, there are many different types and grades of this superb cheese. At the top of the list there is Parmigiano-Reggiano. This is the official Italian name for authentic Parmesan cheese. To carry this name it must be made in the "Zona Tipica," the Provence of Parma and its surrounding areas. In Italy this cheese is often served as a table cheese, split off in good sized chunks and served with fresh fruit as well as the last glass of the same red wine that was served with the main course. After these cheeses are aged for a year, they are stamped and dated as proof of their authenticity. Until you've tasted Parmigiano-Reggiano, you're missing one of the greatest cheeses in the world.

Although Parmigiano-Reggiano is considered the best, Italy also makes other fine grating cheeses called granas. One of the best, produced in the Zona Tipica and not aged quite as long as the Reggiano, is known as Grana Padano; often served as part of an antipasto, it is most often used in cooked dishes.

Romano: The second most famous Italian grating cheese is Romano, made with sheep's milk in the southern part of Italy where sheep are more abundant than cows. This hearty flavored cheese belongs in robust sauces and hearty pasta dishes. Those aged for the longest period of time are called grating Romano, grating Pecorino, and Pecorino Romano, and are available in the United States. Expensive, but worthy of the price, they are marvelous cheeses that can add flavor to any Italian-style food.

HOW TO CHOOSE & BUY CHEESE

When you want really great cheese, begin by finding the best source of supply in your area; it might be a specialty cheese shop, a gourmet takeout food shop, or the cheese section of your supermarket. Whichever one you choose, it should be well stocked with a variety of different cheeses and the sales clerk should be informed and able to answer your questions. It should also be one where business is brisk and there's a fast turnover of merchandise so that you can assume the cheese is fresh and has not been waiting overlong on the shelf.

Cheeses should be wrapped in plastic or an equivalent wrap and kept refrigerated at low temperature in relatively high humidity so they will not lose moisture or ripen too quickly. The only cheeses that should be on the counter are those that the store expects to sell that day and, if the store is cool, hard cheeses that are less susceptible to heat.

In selecting cheeses, remember that good cheeses look good. A cheese you don't know can look unusual or unfamiliar, but it should not look unappetizing.

To choose a good cheese, consider the

following: if you are buying bulk cheese, ask for a sample. One bite is worth a thousand descriptive words.

When buying packaged cheeses, examine the wrapping. It should be fresh and clean without signs of spoilage, such as off odors, stickiness or mold. Soft, ripened cheeses should be plump and fill their boxes.

Blue veined cheeses should be moist and the veins should be in sharp blue or green contrast to the ivory or light yellow color of the cheese. Semi-hard cheeses should have a slightly oily or moist, not dry, surface. Semi-soft cheeses should be tender to the touch.

Strong-flavored cheeses should also be tender, not dry or gummy, and while their smell will be strong and often earthy, it should not be unpleasant.

Fresh chevre cheeses will look light and fluffy. Old chevres become very hard and extremely pungent, a style that certainly has its following, but no chevre, however, should be moldy or evil smelling.

Cremes—double and triple—should have the look of very rich and stiffly beaten heavy cream. They should smell fresh and have an enticing, light fragrance. No creme should have a strong, assertive smell or show signs of mold.

Check the label of cheeses before purchasing them to make sure they are the products you want. All cheeses will show place of origin somewhere on the wrapping. For example, a genuine French Roquefort will have the famous sheep label on its foil covering.

Buy only as much soft-ripened cheese, goat cheese and double or triple creme cheese as you plan to use within a week. Semi-soft, semi-hard and hard cheeses may be stored for longer periods of time.

As soon as you bring your cheeses home, wrap each one separately so that moisture is retained. Place them in the least cold part of the refrigerator; possibly in the fruit or vegetable bin, or on the lower shelves of the refrigerator door.

Always wrap each cheese individually—don't mix varieties. A soft, light tasting cheese can often take on flavor from stronger ones.

It is possible to freeze cheese but because the texture of the frozen cheese tends to become crumbly and its flavor somewhat changed, freezing is not generally recommended.

HOW TO SERVE CHEESE

Cheese tastes best and at its finest when served at room temperature, so take it out of the refrigerator well before you plan to serve it.

Firm and semi-firm cheeses need at least an hour to warm to room temperature. Soft and semi-soft cheeses usually need a half hour or more. Very large pieces of cheese require more time than smaller ones. All cheeses need less time to warm up when the weather is hot. If you plan to serve both hard and soft cheeses, take them out of the refrigerator at different times.

Cheese should be cut according to its shape, so that the rind is evenly distributed and the cheese is easier to keep.

Serve cheeses on simple things—wooden cheese boards, flat wicker baskets and trays, or straw mats. Cheese needs no decoration but if you wish, garnish them with watercress, parsley or add small clusters of grapes.

How many cheeses should you serve? Three to five choices should offer your guests a good variety. Include at least one well known cheese; choose the others from various cheese families.

Arrange the cheeses with enough room between them to make cutting easy. Never place delicately flavored cheese next to strong flavored ones. If possible, have a cheese cutter or knife for each cheese. If not, have one for mild cheeses, one for the medium flavored and one for the strong and sharp. A dinner knife or butter knife can be used for soft and semi-soft cheeses.

CAKES & COOKIES

Listed below are some of the special cookies we have found at our supermarket, bakery and gourmet takeout food shop.

Biscotti: If you've ever vacationed in Italy, you

are undoubtedly already familiar with these crisp and crunchy twice-baked Tuscan-style dipping cookies. Divinely addictive they can be served with or dipped into any beverage from morning coffee to afternoon tea, expresso, or as in Italy, lightly chilled white wine or room temperature red wine, as well as after dinner brandy. Once only an Italian import, they are now made in a family owned bakery in South San Francisco specializing in Italian-style pastries. You'll now find them in almost every specialty food shop as well as many new super-style supermarkets. As they become more readily available, who knows? They may even replace American doughnuts for dunking. For a glamorous dessert break a chocolate covered biscotti into small pieces; place in the bottom of a dessert bowl, heap coffee ice cream on top and drown it all with Kahlua or other coffee liqueur. Or break biscotti with hazelnuts into small pieces, spoon into a dessert bowl and heap raspberry sherbet on top; cover with melba sauce and spoon Framboise (raspberry liqueur) over all.

Chocolate chip cookies: Who can resist them? Though packaged ones can be good, we found the best are freshly baked ones from a top quality bakery. These are more often than not your best and most delicious buy. Made without preservatives and real chocolate chips, they have the fresh taste that, unfortunately, denotes expensive prices.

Chocolate wafers: These crisp, thin, very chocolately chocolate cookies are sometimes hard to find at your supermarket because often they are not placed in the cookie section but near the bottled ice cream dessert sauces. We like to sandwich them with ice cream, use them for a chocolate cookie crumb pie crust, or simply serve them with ice cream. As a bonus, you'll find one of the most delicious and easy to make desserts—made with whipped cream—on the package. When you have time, it's well worth making—a sensational dessert.

Frozen all-butter poundcake: A cake to keep in your freezer at all times, especially when you are expecting "unexpected guests." Top with ice cream and commercially prepared sauce, anything from hot fudge to melba or Nesselrode sauce—impressive, or simply cut this cake into thick slices, spread with butter and sprinkle with brown sugar for an accompaniment to afternoon tea or mid-morning coffee. Cut in layers, poundcake can be frosted with whipped cream or any already prepared frosting. This "anytime" cake can be dressed up or dressed down to suit just about any occasion.

Gauffrettes: At first bite these elegant, very crisp pie-shaped wedges taste like nothing more than an old-fashioned lightly sweetened ice cream cone—the kind you may remember from your childhood—which is basically what they are. However, as you nibble away, you realize the flavor is a little more subtle, more sophisticated and just slightly better than any ice cream cone you've ever experienced. Served with plain ice cream in stemmed wine glasses, they make an elegant ending to a party meal. You'll find them packaged in a decorative tin, one you'll want to keep after the cookies are gone, at most gourmet food shops.

Miniature Irish whiskey cakes & small cakes made with liqueur: These small, four-ounce cakes are the answer to what to serve during the Christmas season. Though you may remember Mama's as being the best holiday cake in the world, what you may be remembering is only the fun of preparing them in leisurely times. You may find these modern cakes even more delicious, especially if you buy them about a month before the season begins. Rip off the top but leave them in their carton and add as much whiskey or liqueur as they can absorb, then rewrap and store them in the refrigerator until ready to serve.

Rolled gauffrettes: Plain or chocolate-tipped, these are very thin, very crisp and very delicious, the best accompaniment to ice cream or a fruit compote you can serve.

Vanilla wafers: Though we never tire of old fashioned vanilla wafers, made with real vanilla, the ones we prefer are not labeled vanilla wafers but brown-edged wafers. They are thinner, more delicious, and as the name implies, circled with crispy brown edges.

JAMS, JELLIES, CONSERVES, PRESERVES, HONEY & SUCH

Honey cream: Honey that has been processed with a thick spreadable paste. One of our new favorite things, though it is still as sticky as all other honeys, it is spreadable—on your morning toast. We mix it with softened butter as a topping for pancakes, waffles and French toast—or we mix it with mustard and serve it with thick slices of deli ham. Mixed with lemon juice, use it as a glaze when reheating takeout rotisserie-broiled chicken halves or roast duck.

Jams & jellies with liqueur: Definitely not for breakfast or even lunch, these heady preserves made with cognac, Grand Marnier, or other liqueur make impressive sauces for vanilla ice cream, custards or puddings.

Lemon curd: This preserve has long been an English teatime treat. Thick and creamy smooth, it has a custard-like texture. The taste is very tart yet sweet. We like to serve it on crisp toast or English muffins for breakfast. For dessert, spread it on poundcake slices, or spoon over ice cream.

Pickled or brandied peaches: Serve these peaches when you want to impress. The pickled kind go particularly well with lunch time salads, especially chicken or shrimp. Brandied peaches can be served as an accompaniment to almost any main course entree, or they can be used to make a classic Peach Melba: place a scoop of vanilla ice cream in a small dessert bowl, top with a peach half and surround with a commercially prepared melba sauce, then top, if you like, with a dollop of whipped cream or triple creme.

Red & green pepper jellies: We first experienced the tart, sweet flavor of these jellies in Charleston, South Carolina where they are locally made and considered a Southern delicacy. Though you can of course serve them with your morning toast, like mint jelly, they are customarily served as an accompaniment to a main course entree. They also make a splendid cocktail appetizer when teamed up with cream cheese and crisp crackers. We suggest you add them to your emergency shelf as a go-with for Southern fried chicken or ribs. Mixed with mustard they make a splendid sauce to serve with cold meats.

Unsweetened berry conserves: These pure, unsweetened, fruit only, jam-like preserves contain no artificial sweeteners. They are made with fruit and unsweetened grape, apple and lemon juices from concentrate, plus fruit pectin. We love their tart, sweet flavor. They are great with croissants or English muffins, or use as a topping for ice cream or filling for cake layers and bakery-made tart shells.

Watermelon rind pickles: Crisp, crunchy and not too sweet, here's another Southern specialty that can make special a platter of baked Virginia ham, turn chicken or tuna salad into a mouthwatering meal or can be used as a go-with for rotisserie-broiled chicken or roast duck.

COMMERCIALLY PREPARED DESSERT SAUCES

Ice cream toppings—chocolate, hot fudge, caramel, strawberry & other fruit sauces: Definitely easier and quicker to buy than to make; new ones, found in the gourmet section of your supermarket, can be very definitely better than when home prepared. Serve them, of course, over ice cream or fold them into whipped cream. Sandwich them between thin slices of poundcake and top with sweetened whipped cream. Spoon them over freshly prepared French toast and serve for a festive brunch, or fold into a sweet dessert omelet.

Melba sauce, Nesselrode sauce, brandied fruit: Though these exceptionally delicious sauces can be made in your own kitchen, we found, after testing, that even when we could find all the necessary ingredients the prepared variety proved not only less expensive but equally if not superior in flavor. Any one of them can transform plain ice cream or fresh fruit into an elegant and seductive dessert. In addition, they can all be used in any number of very festive desserts. Leftovers can be stored in the refrigerator almost indefinitely.

LAST BUT NOT LEAST, CHOCOLATE

We're not going to tell you that a chocolate dessert is still just about everyone's favorite. You are probably already well aware of this fact, but we remind you, you don't have to make it—you can buy it. In addition to the many wonderful chocolate cakes and cookies you'll find at your favorite bakery, consider the following options:

Chocolate dessert shells: These ready-to-fill (2-3/4" x 1") shells are large enough to fill with ice cream, sherbet or fresh berries, or they can also be used to hold a number of different puddings and custards. For example, see the recipe for Chocolate Pecan Tarts and its variations.

Chocolate truffles: Buy the jumbo-size ones you'll now find at the candy department of most gourmet-type takeout food shops. Simply cut them crosswise into slices, arrange the slices on small dessert plates and sprinkle them very lightly with a little brandy or rum.

Miniature foil-wrapped chocolates: Arrange them in one layer on a large platter or plate and serve in the living room along with freshly brewed, after-dinner coffee. This allows you a few minutes to clear off the dining room table, straighten up the kitchen and join your guests before they have time to realize you have completed this chore.

PAWLEYS ISLAND
BACK PORCH SHRIMP BOIL

Set your back porch, patio, or kitchen table with a colorful plastic or paper tablecloth—use brightly colored plastic or paper plates. Beside each plate place a small bowl to hold shrimp shells. Provide a salad fork and a small sharp knife to remove peel from shrimp. Place all prepared food on the table and let everyone peel their own shrimp and help themselves.

Pawleys Island Back Porch Shrimp Boil, see below

Potato salad from the deli

Cole slaw from the deli

Chili sauce & tartar sauce

Crisp assorted pickles

Platter of sliced tomatoes sprinkled with

vinaigrette dressing

Beer or light ale

Freshly-made coffee and crisp cookies from the bakery

Pawleys Island Back Porch Shrimp Boil

2 pints beer or light ale
1 pint water
2 tablespoons packaged shrimp boil
6 jumbo or 9 to 12 medium raw shrimp for each serving

Pour beer, water and shrimp boil into a large heavy pot over medium heat. Bring to a boil; reduce heat and let simmer about 10 minutes. Add unpeeled shrimp, stir once, cover and let steam until shells are bright pink, 3 to 4 minutes. Drain into a colander; transfer to a large flat straw basket or a colorful flat tin tray. Serve at room temperature.

TACO BUFFET PARTY

Here's a terrific no-work way of entertaining! Everyone has fun assembling and eating tacos. The beef filling mixture can be spooned into a colorful fondue pot or electric skillet and placed on the table just before the party begins. Toppings can be set out in small wooden bowls or glazed Mexican pottery bowls.

Use fat candles in Mexican tin candlesticks or colorful ceramic ones to light up the table and complete the effect with a centerpiece of fresh yellow daisies. Surround, if you like, with colorful papier-maché animals, the kind you'll find at Mexican gift shops. Serve imported Mexican beer as the beverage. Dessert can be as simple as a large bowl filled with icy cold green grapes, Mexican-style praline candy and freshly brewed coffee.

Beef-bean mixture from Taco Salad, page 137

Guacamole from Guacamole Salad, page 131

Refried beans (takeout or canned)

Warmed flour and corn tortillas

Shredded Monterey Jack cheese

Shredded Longhorn cheese

Chopped tomatoes   Diced onions

Thinly sliced radishes   Sliced mushrooms

Diced celery   Sliced ripe olives

Stuffed green olives   Dairy sour cream

Mild and hot salsas

Green grapes

Mexican-style praline candy

Coffee and Beer

APPETIZERS & SNACKS

The easiest way to transform a simple entree into a party meal is to begin with a festive appetizer. Not only does it give the instant gourmet host or hostess time to prepare the main course of the meal, it also allows the guests time to unwind with a predinner drink.

Almost all of the appetizers and snacks to follow can be served with drinks before the meal, or as part of a buffet supper party. Some are so simple they can be prepared at the last minute, others can be prepared ahead of time. In addition, if you are late from work or wherever and you don't have to time to prepare even a simple dip, I've included quite a few "recipes" that encourage people to "make their own." Just assemble all of the required ingredients on one attractive serving platter or plate, then place them on a tray or table accessible to everyone. In addition to being a time and work saver, it's also a way to start the conversation going and get the party off to a good start.

A smooth, rich mixture. Serve with crisp unsalted crackers, melba toast or toasted bread.

TEN MINUTE PÂTÉ MAISON

1/2 lb. liverwurst, room temperature

1/4 cup butter, room temperature

1 to 2 tablespoons thick gourmet-type steak sauce

1 to 2 teaspoons Dijon-style or similar mustard

2 to 3 tablespoons cognac or other brandy

1 tablespoon minced parsley

1/4 teaspoon coarsely ground black pepper

Place liverwurst and butter in a small bowl; mash with a fork until smooth. Blend in steak sauce, mustard, brandy and parsley; season with pepper. Form mixture into a ball. Makes about 2 cups pâté.

Variation
Grease a 2-cup non-decorative mold with 1 teaspoon butter; sprinkle with 1 tablespoon minced parsley, rotating mold to distribute evenly. Spoon pâté into mold. Cover mold with plastic wrap; refrigerate several hours or until firm. To serve, dip bottom of mold briefly into hot water. Unmold onto a small serving plate.

Serving suggestions: Serve with crisp vegetables, assorted crackers and breads, cheeses and fruit for a quick appetizer party. Include a light wine, soft drinks or punch.

Of course you can make these elegant little canapes yourself, but why not let your guests make their own? It's fun and a great way to get the party conversation off to a smooth start.

MAKE-YOUR-OWN SMOKED SALMON CANAPES

1 pkg. cocktail rye bread rounds

1 (8-oz.) pkg. cream cheese with chives

1/2 lb. thinly sliced smoked salmon, cut in narrow strips

Arrange bread in an attractive straw basket or on a bread board. Place cream cheese on a small platter or plate. Arrange salmon strips around cheese; bring both to living room and place on coffee table or other easy to reach table. Provide butter spreader for cheese and small cocktail fork for salmon. Makes 4 to 6 servings.

It only takes a few minutes to prepare these "knock-em dead" bite-size appetizers.

STUFFED CHERRY TOMATOES

1 (3-oz.) pkg. cream cheese, room temperature

About 1/2 (2-oz.) jar red salmon caviar

8 large cherry tomatoes

Place cream cheese in a small bowl; gently stir in caviar. Cut each tomato in half; gently squeeze out seeds. With a small spoon, stuff tomato halves with cream cheese mixture. If desired, refrigerate until ready to serve. Makes 16 appetizers.

You can serve these shrimp with lemon wedges as a first course or serve them over a bed of rice as a light main course luncheon dish. Though the way we prepare them takes a few minutes longer than other similar recipes, there's much less danger of overcooking the shrimp simply to cook the bacon.

GRILLED SHRIMP IN BACON

16 jumbo shrimp

8 lean bacon strips

Lemon wedges, optional

Hot cooked rice, optional

Drop unpeeled shrimp into a large pot of rapidly boiling water; boil until shells turn pink, about 2 minutes. Drain, cool slightly, then peel and devein. Place bacon in single layer in a large-size heavy skillet over low heat until quite a bit of fat has been rendered but the bacon is still limp. Drain strips briefly on paper towels, then cut each in half. Wrap each shrimp in a bacon strip and thread on skewers. Place about 4 inches from heat source; cook, turning once or twice, until bacon is crisp, about 2 minutes on each side. Serve with lemon wedges as a first course or serve with rice as a main course entree. Makes 4 servings.

You can serve these delectable shrimp in a chafing dish or electric skillet as part of a buffet supper, or as the first course of an impressive dinner party.

GRILLED SHRIMP IN GARLIC BUTTER

1/4 lb. unsalted butter

Dash of garlic juice

1/2 cup lime or lemon juice

Salt and freshly ground pepper

16 jumbo shrimp, peeled, deveined

1/4 cup finely minced parsley

About 1/3 cup mild salsa

Toast points, optional

Place broiler rack about 3 inches from broiler heat or preheat electric grill. Melt butter in a small saucepan over low heat; stir in garlic juice and lime juice. Season lightly with salt and pepper. Briefly dip each shrimp in mixture, letting it drain over saucepan. Place on a broiler pan or preheated grill; broil or grill until shrimp are lightly charred and coral pink, about 2 minutes. Transfer shrimp and remaining butter mixture into an electric skillet, set on low. Sprinkle with minced parsley. Spoon salsa into a small bowl; provide decorative food picks for spearing shrimp and dipping in sauce. For a seated dinner party, spoon butter sauce onto rimmed plates; top with shrimp. Sprinkle with parsley. Spoon a small mound of salsa in the center of each plate. Serve with toast points, if desired. Makes 8 to 16 appetizer servings or 4 as a first course entree.

Serve on French bread rounds from a long thin loaf, crisp unsalted crackers or cocktail rye bread rounds.

TAPENADE

1 (2-oz.) can anchovy fillets in olive oil

1/2 (6-1/2-oz.) jar imported olive spread (olivata)

2 to 3 tablespoons lemon juice

Olive oil, if desired

Freshly ground black pepper

Place anchovies with oil in a medium-size bowl; mash with a fork until smooth. Stir in olive spread and lemon juice. Add more lemon juice or oil to taste. Season generously with pepper. Makes about 1/2 cup tapenade.

Easy to make, wonderful to eat with sparkling white wine or any other predinner drink.

FRESH FIGS WITH HAM

8 large ripe figs

Lemon juice

Freshly ground black pepper

6 narrow strips Westphalian, Black Forest or prosciutto ham, fat removed

Peel each fig, roll each in lemon juice, then sprinkle with pepper. Wrap each in a thin strip of ham; secure with a wooden pick. Makes 8 appetizer servings.

It's an appetizer sandwich on a stick! Serve with raw vegetables and cheeses for an easy appetizer party.

HAM ROLL-UPS

1 (3-oz.) pkg. cream cheese, room temperature

2 to 3 teaspoons half and half

12 very thin slices (about 2" x 4") flavorful ham, such as Westphalian, Black Forest or proscuitto

12 crissini (long thin Italian-style bread sticks)

Place cream cheese in a small bowl; add sufficient cream to make a thick spreading consistency. Spread each slice of ham with cheese mixture. Roll each slice, cheese side in, diagonally around crissini. If desired, refrigerate for about 1 hour before serving. Makes 12.

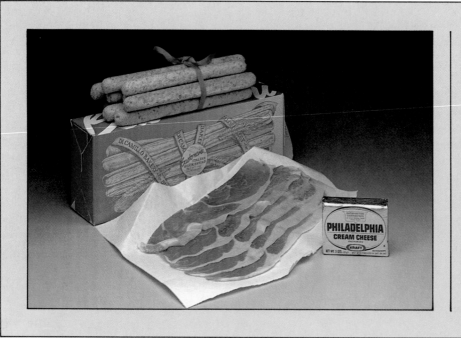

Serving suggestions: A chilled light wine such as white zinfandel is a perfect wine to serve with this for a summer party.

Rare roast beef slices spread with a flavorful mix of olive spread and mustard.

ROAST BEEF SAN REMO

1 tablespoon Dijon-style mustard

3/4 cup imported olive spread (olivata)

24 thin rare roast beef slices, about 3/4 lb.

Paprika

Hard-cooked egg wedges, optional

Parsley sprigs, optional

In a medium-size bowl, combine mustard and olive spread, blending well. Spread each roast beef slice with olive mixture; loosely roll up. Arrange rolls in a single layer on a long serving platter; sprinkle lightly with paprika. If desired, garnish platter with egg wedges and parsley sprigs. Makes 6 servings.

Serve this appetizing mixture with crisp crackers as a "go-with" for predinner drinks.

PESTO CHEESE WHIP

1 (16-oz.) carton low-fat ricotta cheese

4 to 6 radishes, chopped

1 to 2 tablespoons minced fresh chives

1 to 2 tablespoons pesto sauce

1 tablespoon cider vinegar

Salt and freshly ground pepper

Place cheese in medium-size bowl; stir in remaining ingredients. Serve at once or cover and refrigerate until ready to use. Makes about 2-1/2 cups.

This quick version of an Italian classic is lighter, fresher and more flavorful than the original.

PEPERONATA ITALIAN-AMERICAN STYLE

2 large green bell peppers, cut in 1/4-inch strips

2 large red bell peppers, cut in 1/4-inch strips

1 large tomato, peeled, seeded, chopped

1 small Vidalia or red onion, peeled, chopped

1/4 cup avocado oil or light and fruity olive oil

Salt and freshly ground pepper

Place bell peppers in a large heavy skillet; pour in sufficient water to cover by about 1 inch. Bring to a boil. Boil until crisp-tender, about 1 minute. Drain into a colander, then transfer to a long shallow glass dish. Add tomato and onion; stir in oil. Season lightly with salt and pepper. Let stand at room temperature until ready to serve. Drain just before serving. Makes 4 to 6 appetizer servings.

This is not one, but a number of different appetizers that take less time to put together than the telling. Serve with butter knives and let each guest make his or her own. Each makes about 8 servings.

CREAM CHEESE APPETIZERS

CHARLESTON-STYLE

1 (8-oz.) pkg. cream cheese, room temperature

About 1/2 cup green pepper jelly

Place cream cheese in center of a serving plate. Spoon jelly on top, letting excess fall onto plate. Serve with unsalted water biscuits or commercially prepared beaten biscuits.

ITALIAN-STYLE

1 (8-oz.) carton ricotta cheese, drained

1 (6-oz.) jar Italian-style mushroom salad

Mound ricotta cheese in center of a serving plate. Top with mushroom salad, letting excess fall onto plate. Serve with Italian-style bread wedges.

A LA FRANÇAISE

1 (4- to 6-oz.) log Bucheron (goat cheese)

1 (2-oz.) jar red salmon caviar

Place Bucheron on a serving plate. Top with caviar, letting excess fall onto plate. Serve with thinly sliced bread from a long, thin and crusty French-style loaf.

SOUTH OF THE BORDER

8 oz. Monterey Jack cheese, cut in thin slices

About 1/2 cup salsa

Place slices of cheese in the center of a serving plate. Surround with salsa. Serve with crisp large, thick tortilla chips.

Serve as a very "classy" first course or as a separate salad with or after the main course.

GRILLED CHEVRES WITH AVOCADO OIL

1 small head Boston or Bibb lettuce, shredded

2 tablespoons avocado oil or vegetable oil

1 tablespoon white wine vinegar

Salt and freshly ground pepper

4 small (3-1/2- to 4-oz.) round goat cheeses

Thin bread slices from a long narrow French loaf or crisp unsalted crackers

Place broiler rack about 4 inches from heat. Preheat broiler to high. In a large bowl, combine lettuce, oil and vinegar; season with salt and pepper. Toss to mix, set aside. Place the cheeses on a baking sheet. Broil just until tops are lightly browned and heated through. Place each on 1 side of a salad plate; place salad mixture on other side. Serve with bread or crackers. Makes 4 servings.

SUMMER SQUASH PIZZA ROUNDS

2 large round yellow "summer" squash

About 1 tablespoon olive oil

About 1/2 cup bottled taco sauce

About 2 tablespoons shredded or chopped mozzarella cheese

5 sliced, pitted Niçoise olives

Preheat oven to 350F (175C). Trim ends from squash and discard. Cut squash crosswise into about 1/4-inch-thick slices. With your fingers or a pastry brush, coat both sides of each slice very lightly with olive oil; place in single layer on a baking sheet. Spoon 1/2 to 1 teaspoon taco sauce in center of each. Top sauce with about 1/4 teaspoon cheese and an olive slice. Bake in preheated oven 5 to 6 minutes, or until topping is hot and cheese is partially melted. Makes 16 to 18.

Variation
Substitute 8 or 9 miniature patty pan squash for larger squash. Cut in half crosswise. Trim ends so slices set flat.

Serving suggestions: A light red wine goes well with this pizza-without-a-crust. To carry out the Italian theme, add the crudités from page 53 and Italian breadsticks.

Though carrot sticks and green pepper strips may go begging, these flavorful appetizers seem to vanish as quickly as they appear.

STUFFED MUSHROOMS

About 1/4 cup lemon juice

About 1/2 cup water

12 jumbo fresh mushrooms

About 1 cup stuffing mixture, see below

Minced parsley, paprika or freshly ground black pepper, optional

In a small bowl, combine lemon juice and water. Gently twist stems from mushrooms caps; reserve for other use or mince and add to mushroom filling mixture. Wipe caps clean with damp paper towels; dip into bowl containing lemon-water. Use a small spoon to stuff each with any of the mixtures below, mounding mixture high, then smoothing it with back of spoon. If desired, sprinkle with minced parsley, paprika or freshly ground black pepper. Makes 12 appetizers.

Each stuffing mixture below is enough for 12 large mushrooms caps.

ROQUEFORT CHEESE FILLING

4 oz. Roquefort cheese, room temperature

1 (3-oz.) pkg. cream cheese, room temperature

1/2 teaspoon dry mustard

In a small bowl, combine ingredients; beat with a fork until well blended.

CHEVRE FILLING WITH WALNUTS

6 oz. Montrachet (mild goat cheese), room temperature

1 tablespoon whipping cream

2 oz. walnuts, ground

Place cheese in a small bowl, add cream and beat until smooth. Stir in walnuts.

CREAM CHEESE HORSERADISH FILLING

1 (8-oz.) pkg. cream cheese, room temperature

1 tablespoon dairy sour cream

2 teaspoons prepared horseradish

1 tablespoon minced chives

In a small bowl, combine cream cheese, sour cream and horseradish; beat until smooth. Stir in minced chives.

CREAM CHEESE & SMITHFIELD HAM FILLING

1 (3-oz.) pkg. cream cheese, room temperature

2 tablespoons dairy sour cream

1/4 cup Smithfield ham spread

In a small bowl, combine cream cheese, sour cream and ham spread. Beat with a fork until well blended.

These elegant looking little soufflés make an impressive first course for a party meal.

INDIVIDUAL CHEESE SOUFFLÉS

1 cup (4 oz.) shredded Cheddar cheese

1 (3-oz.) pkg. cream cheese, room temperature

1 egg yolk

1 tablespoon butter, room temperature

6 egg whites

Paprika

Lightly grease 6 (3-inch) porcelain or ceramic soufflé dishes with butter. Preheat oven to 400F (205C). Combine Cheddar cheese, cream cheese and egg yolk in a large bowl. Beat until light and fluffy. In a separate bowl, beat egg whites until stiff peaks form. Fold beaten egg whites, about 1/4 at a time, into cheese mixture. Spoon into prepared molds. Sprinkle with paprika. Bake in preheated oven until well puffed and lightly browned, about 10 minutes. Serve immediately. Makes 6 servings.

No one need know how little time you spent in the kitchen preparing these addictive appetizers.

MINIATURE QUICHE

1 (3-oz.) package cream cheese, room temperature

4 oz. feta cheese, room temperature

1 egg

1/4 cup grated Parmesan cheese

2 or 3 drops hot pepper sauce

3 tablespoons Italian seasoned bread crumbs

3 tablespoons mango chutney

Preheat oven to 375F (190C). In a medium-size bowl, beat cream cheese and feta cheese with egg, Parmesan cheese and hot pepper sauce until light and fluffy. Line 12-cup miniature (1-3/4 inch in diameter) muffin pans with paper baking cups. Place about 1 teaspoon of seasoned crumbs in bottom of each cup. Fill cups with cream cheese mixture, dividing evenly. Top each with about 1 teaspoon of mango chutney. Bake in preheated oven 10 minutes. Cool in pans on rack to room temperature. Makes 12 miniature quiches.

This creamy filling stretches expensive proscuitto for a dinner party first course. Serve with lightly buttered rye bread rounds or hot buttered toast points.

PROSCIUTTO ROLLS WITH SOUR CREAM FILLING

1 (3-oz.) pkg. cream cheese, room temperature

1 tablespoon dairy sour cream

1/4 cup minced parsley or chives

6 long very thin slices prosciutto

Parsley sprigs

In a small bowl, combine cream cream and sour cream; mix with a fork until well blended. Stir in parsley. Spread mixture on ham slices and roll up. Refrigerate until chilled. Cut rolls across into thick slices. Arrange slices on small appetizer or salad plates and garnish with parsley. Makes 4 servings.

Very few people can tell "what's in it" when tasting this delicious dip.

MYSTERY INGREDIENT DIP

1 (13-3/4-oz.) can water packed artichoke bottoms, drained

1 cup mayonnaise

1 cup (3 oz.) grated Parmesan cheese

Thick potato chips, taco chips, optional

Preheat oven to 400F (205C). Lightly butter a 3-cup heatproof baking dish. Place artichoke bottoms in work bowl of food processor; process until finely chopped (or place on chopping board and chop with knife). In a large bowl, combine chopped artichokes, mayonnaise and cheese; transfer to buttered baking dish. Bake in preheated oven until bubbly and edges are lightly browned, about 10 minutes. Serve hot or at room temperature with large, thick potato chips or taco chips. Makes about 2 cups.

This colorful mix of crisp cooked vegetables, shiny black olives and deep green pickles can be served as the first course of a meal or as part of a buffet table menu. The surprise ingredient in this festive platter is crunchy, colorful pickled baby corn. Once found only in Oriental dishes, it has suddenly begun to appear in the gourmet department of your supermarket.

CRUDITÉS WITH GARLICKY SOUR CREAM DIP

Garlicky Sour Cream Dip, see opposite

1/2 lb. miniature carrots

1/2 lb. broccoli flowerets

1/2 lb. cauliflowerets

2 to 3 tablespoons lemon juice

1/4 cup top-quality extra virgin olive oil

Salt

1/4 lb. pitted Niçoise olives from deli

1 (5-oz.) jar pickled baby corn, drained

Parsley sprigs

GARLICKY SOUR CREAM DIP

1/2 pint dairy sour cream

1 teaspoon garlic paste

1 teaspoon hot Hungarian paprika

Salt

Prepare Garlicky Sour Cream Dip as directed below. Cover and refrigerate until chilled or ready to serve. Place carrots on steamer rack in a steamer pot over simmering water; cover and steam about 2 minutes. Add broccoli flowerets, steam 1 minute, then add cauliflowerets and steam 1 minute. Transfer vegetables to a colander; rinse under cold running water to set color and cool slightly. Transfer to a bowl; stir in lemon juice and olive oil. Season lightly with salt. Let vegetables stand at room temperature about 1 hour or cover and refrigerate for several hours or until ready to serve. To serve, drain off and discard liquid from vegetables. Add olives and corn; stir to mix. Place Garlicky Sour Cream Dip in the center of a large round plate or platter; surround with vegetable mixture and garnish with parsley sprigs. Serves 6 or 8 as a first course; 8 to 12 as part of a buffet party menu.

GARLICKY SOUR CREAM DIP

In a small bowl, combine ingredients and stir to mix thoroughly. Cover and refrigerate until chilled or ready to serve. Spoon into a small serving bowl. Dip may be made up to 1 day ahead. Makes about 1 cup.

SOUPS

The soups we present here are all proof positive that less can indeed be more. All are deliciously nourishing yet none take more time to prepare, well almost, than the telling. The image of a large pot of simmering stock on the back of your stove is passe. Though stock can indeed enrich and add nourishment to any soup, you no longer have to make it yourself; it can be purchased at just about all gourmet-type takeout food shops as well as at many supermarkets. You'll find it conveniently packaged in small quantities in the freezer section. Use it, as we have done, in many of the recipes to follow, or use it to create your own favorite soup. It's very easy, simple and quick. All you need do is to place 2 to 4 ounces of frozen stock in a saucepan, add 3 to 4 cups water plus a can of chicken or beef broth and bring to a simmer, stirring occasionally. Add, if you like, a small quantity of fresh, frozen or canned vegetables, deli-prepared or leftover home cooked meats, poultry or seafood. The resulting magic comes from your own good taste and your understanding of what goes with what.

To be honest, the recipes you'll find here are not totally original but simply quick and easy adaptations of classics that have pleased and nourished many generations. They can be served in small quantities as a first course or, as we have become more interested in light eating, as a main course entree. We like to serve them with hearty breads and sometimes with a wedge of Brie or Camembert plus a glass of light wine. Served hot these soups can banish the cold of a wintry day; chilled, they make an excellent choice for a summer luncheon or supper party.

"Soup is cuisine's kindest course" is an old saying. Now, in addition, it is also the easiest and simplest of all classic cookery.

This pale pink soup looks especially appetizing in pale pink and white tulip-shaped cups.

SHRIMP BISQUE

1 (2-oz.) container frozen fish and lobster stock concentrate

2-1/2 cups half and half

1/2 lb. raw shrimp, peeled, deveined

1/4 cup dry sherry

Salt and pepper

Minced chives or parsley

Place stock and half and half in a large heavy saucepan. Cook over low heat until stock is melted and mixture is smooth. Add shrimp, reduce heat and simmer about 3 minutes. Stir in sherry; simmer about 2 minutes. Remove from heat. Scoop out shrimp and about 1 cup liquid; place in work bowl of food processor or blender. Process until shrimp are finely minced; stir shrimp back into remaining mixture in saucepan. Stir over medium heat until hot. Season with salt and pepper. Ladle into soup bowls or mugs; sprinkle with chives. Makes 2 main course servings or 3 or 4 first course servings.

This is a delightful soup for entertaining. Serve it in small deep soup bowls accompanied by small thin slices of French bread.

OYSTER BISQUE

1 quart small oysters and their liquid

1 quart (4 cups) half and half

2 tablespoons butter

2 tablespoons sherry, optional

1/2 cup soft white bread crumbs

Salt and pepper

Minced fresh or thawed frozen chives

Place oysters and their liquid in work bowl of food processor or blender. Process until oysters are chopped. Heat half and half in a large heavy saucepan over low heat until hot. Stir in butter and, if desired, sherry. When butter melts, add oysters and liquid. Stir in bread crumbs; cook, stirring, about 5 minutes. Remove saucepan from heat; cover and let soup stand about 10 minutes. Return saucepan to low heat; cook, stirring, until hot. Season with salt and pepper. If desired, sprinkle with chives. Makes 6 to 8 servings.

We prefer to serve this soup as a main course entree followed by a tossed green salad with a wedge of Brie, then end the meal with a light but festive dessert.

LOBSTER-CRAB BISQUE

2 (2-oz.) containers frozen fish and lobster stock concentrate

1 (10-3/4-oz.) can condensed seafood bisque

1 soup can half and half

1 (6-oz.) pkg. frozen King crabmeat, thawed, drained, or 1 cup fresh crabmeat

Salt and pepper

1-1/2 to 2 cups cold cooked rice

Paprika, optional

Place frozen stock in a large saucepan over medium heat until thawed. Stir in soup and half and half; cook, stirring, until hot. Stir in crabmeat. Season with salt and pepper. Place rice in a colander; rinse under hot water. Ladle soup into 4 large shallow soup bowls; place a scoop of the rice in the center of each bowl. If desired, sprinkle rice lightly with paprika. Makes 4 servings.

I think you'll like the combination of flavors and textures in this earthy yet elegant soup.

CORN & SEAFOOD BISQUE

2 tablespoons butter

1 small Vidalia onion or purple onion, chopped

1 tablespoon all-purpose flour

1/2 teaspoon curry powder

1 pint (2 cups) half and half

1 (10-oz.) pkg. frozen "Shoe Peg" white corn kernels

Any one of the following: 1/2 lb. frozen or fresh lump crabmeat, fresh bay scallops, peeled and deveined cooked shrimp, tiny frozen "popcorn" shrimp

Salt and pepper

Melt butter in a large saucepan or soup pot; add onion. Sauté about 1 minute or until softened. Stir in flour and curry powder; cook, stirring, until bubbly. Add half and half and corn; cook, stirring, until hot. Stir in seafood. Season with salt and pepper. Serve at once in deep soup bowls. Makes 4 servings.

True Dover sole is very difficult to find in this country, because it must be imported from France or England. Sole in the United States is usually lemon or gray sole, either of which will work very well in this delicious soup.

CREAMY SOLE-CHIVE SOUP

2 (2-oz.) containers frozen concentrated fish and lobster stock

2-1/2 cups water

1/2 cup dry white wine

1 lb. fresh sole fillets, cut in narrow strips

1 teaspoon herbs de Provence

Salt

1 cup half and half

Chopped chives

Place frozen stock in a wide, deep, non-aluminum saucepan; add water and wine. Cook, stirring, over medium heat until stock has dissolved completely and mixture comes to a full boil. Add fish; cook, stirring, until each forms a "corkscrew," about 30 seconds. Scoop out fish with a slotted spoon; place in a heated soup tureen or individual soup bowls, dividing evenly. Add remaining ingredients to soup pot; bring mixture back to a boil, stirring. Pour soup over fish; sprinkle with chives. Serve at once. Makes 6 to 8 servings.

We were served this bracing hot broth mid-morning on board the Queen Elizabeth during a wintertime crossing.

CLEAR BEEF BROTH, QUEEN ELIZABETH STYLE

2 (2-oz.) containers frozen beef stock concentrate

2 cups water

Dash of Worcestershire sauce

1 teaspoon lemon juice

1 tablespoon concentrated Bloody Mary mix

Salt and pepper

Place frozen stock in a medium-size saucepan; add water. Stir over medium heat until stock has thawed. Add Worcestershire sauce, lemon juice and Bloody Mary mix; season with salt and pepper. Bring to a simmer. Pour into heatproof mugs; serve at once. Makes 4 to 6 servings.

This elegant soup can be served hot or cold. Either way, the flavor is exceptional.

CREAM OF ASPARAGUS SOUP WITH PESTO

1 (10-1/2 oz.) can cut green asparagus spears, drained

1 (10-3/4-oz.) can condensed chicken broth

2 tablespoons pesto sauce

1 cup half and half

1 to 2 dashes hot pepper sauce

1/4 teaspoon dried Italian herbs

Salt

1/4 cup minced fresh or frozen chives

Place asparagus in work bowl of food processor or blender. Add 1/4 of the chicken broth and the pesto sauce. Process until mixture is almost but not quite smooth (small pieces and flecks of asparagus should remain visible). Pour mixture into a medium saucepan; place over low heat. Stir in remaining broth, half and half, hot pepper sauce and herbs. Cook, stirring, until hot. Season with salt to taste. Serve hot or pour into storage container; refrigerate until chilled or ready to serve. (Soup can be prepared up to 1 day ahead.) Serve soup in small bowls. Sprinkle each serving with chives. Makes 2 generous servings as a light main course or 4 first course servings.

Serving suggestions: For a summer evening, serve this soup chilled as the first course. Follow with the salmon salad on page 138 and French bread for a meal that's sure to beat the heat.

This soup has superb flavor but very few calories.

SESAME MUSHROOM SOUP, ORIENTAL STYLE

2 teaspoons corn or other vegetable oil

1/2 teaspoon Oriental sesame oil

1/4 lb. mushrooms, chopped

1 (14-1/2-oz.) can regular strength chicken broth

1 tablespoon minced chives

1/2 to 1 teaspoon Oriental sesame oil

Heat corn oil and 1/2 teaspoon sesame oil in a large saucepan over medium heat. When hot, add mushrooms; cook, stirring, about 30 seconds, then cover and let steam 2 to 3 minutes or until mushrooms have given off some of their liquid. Pour in broth; cook, stirring occasionally, until liquid comes to a simmer. Remove saucepan from heat and stir in chives. Pour into soup bowls or mugs. Drizzle each serving with a few drops of sesame oil and serve at once. Makes 2 large or 4 small servings.

A mid-summer special.

CREAMY GAZPACHO

1-1/2 cups tomato juice

1 tablespoon mild virgin olive oil

1 tablespoon red wine vinegar

2 to 3 drops garlic juice

Salt and coarsely ground black pepper

1 large firm ripe tomato, seeded, coarsely chopped

1 small cucumber, peeled, seeded, coarsely chopped

1 small Vidalia or other mild onion, coarsely chopped

About 1/2 cup dairy sour cream

Thin cucumber slices

Watercress sprigs

Place tomato juice, oil, vinegar and garlic juice in work bowl of food processor or blender; season lightly with salt and pepper. Process until smooth. Add tomato, chopped cucumber and onion; process until chopped. Transfer to a large bowl. Stir in enough sour cream to lightly coat vegetables; refrigerate until chilled. Pour into small serving bowls. Garnish with cucumber slices and watercress; serve at once. Makes 4 servings.

The fresh broccoli gives this canned soup its made-from-scratch flavor.

BROCCOLI, BROCCOLI SOUP

1/4 lb. broccoli flowerets

1/2 cup chicken broth

1 (10-3/4-oz.) can cream of broccoli soup

1 soup can of half and half, room temperature

1 to 2 tablespoons dairy sour cream, room temperature, optional

Grated Parmesan cheese, optional

Coarsely chop broccoli; place in a large saucepan with broth. Cook over low heat until crisp-tender, about 3 minutes. Stir in soup and half and half; cook, stirring, until steamy hot. If desired, stir in sour cream. Ladle into soup bowls or mugs; serve very hot. If desired, pass a small bowl of grated cheese so that everyone can sprinkle cheese over soup to taste. Makes 4 to 6 servings.

Variation

Prepare cauliflower soup using cauliflower and cream of cauliflower soup as directed above. Sprinkle with paprika just before serving.

You can serve this soup cold or hot—but do serve it—whenever you need a nourishing, bracing pick-me-up.

INSTANT CREAMY SPINACH SOUP

1/2 (10-oz.) pkg. (about 5 oz.) frozen chopped spinach

1 large tomato, peeled, seeded, chopped

1 cup chicken or beef broth

1/2 cup half and half

Dash of hot pepper sauce

Salt and pepper

Place frozen spinach in a colander; rinse under hot running water for a few seconds. Break slightly thawed spinach into small chunks. Place in work bowl of food processor or blender; add remaining ingredients. Process until mixture is smooth. If necessary, correct seasoning with additional salt and pepper. Pour into small bowls and serve at once or pour mixture into a saucepan and stir until heated. Ladle hot soups into deep mugs. Makes 2 servings.

This soup contains only four basic ingredients and takes less than 10 minutes to prepare.

HOT & SPICY TOMATO SOUP

1 (16-oz.) can Italian imported whole plum tomatoes

1 cup half and half

2 tablespoons dairy sour cream

1 tablespoon concentrated Bloody Mary mix

Salt

Dairy sour cream

Minced chives or parsley

Drain tomatoes, reserving juice. Place tomatoes, 1/2 cup tomato juice, half and half, 2 tablespoons sour cream and Bloody Mary mix in work bowl of food processor or blender. Process until tomatoes are minced. Transfer to a large saucepan. Cook over medium heat, stirring, until hot. Season with salt. Ladle into 4 soup bowls and, if desired, top each serving with a dollop of dairy sour cream and sprinkle with chives or parsley. Makes 4 servings.

Serving suggestions: Start the meal with this easy soup. Then serve one of the Dinners on a Plate for a delicious meal that will get you out of the kitchen in just minutes.

The secret of this superb soup is slow cooking—nonetheless, it still belongs in the instant gourmet's file of great recipes as you will undoubtedly see when you read the directions.

FRENCH ONION SOUP

1 tablespoon butter

1 tablespoon corn oil or other vegetable oil

1 large Vidalia onion, chopped

1 (14-1/2-oz.) can regular strength beef broth

1 tablespoon dry sherry, optional

Dash of hot pepper sauce, optional

Grated Parmesan cheese

In a large, heavy, deep skillet, heat butter and oil over very low heat. Add onion; cook about 15 minutes or until tender and deep golden in color. Increase heat to medium high; pour in beef broth and, if desired, sherry and hot pepper sauce. Let mixture simmer until very hot. Ladle into individual soup cups or small earthenware bowls, dividing evenly. Sprinkle with Parmesan cheese. Makes 2 large or 4 small servings.

Some like it hot, some like it cold. Either way, it is equally delicious.

APPLE CURRY SOUP

1 small tart apple

1 (10-3/4-oz.) can condensed chicken consomme

1 soup can half and half

1 to 2 teaspoons curry powder or to taste

Salt and pepper

Peel, core and chop apple; place in work bowl of food processor or blender. Add 1/2 of the consomme; process until smooth. Transfer to a medium-size bowl; stir in remaining consomme and half and half; season to taste with curry powder, salt and pepper. Makes 4 to 6 small servings.

MEATS

I like to cook. For me, it's a pleasurable activity. I enjoy spending time in my kitchen, but only when I have leisure time to do so. What I don't like and no longer will do is rush home from my office after a day at work and prepare a meal from start to finish. I'm sure you feel much the same way. That is why I now incorporate many commercially prepared and gourmet takeout foods into my menus. They free me to do my own job much more efficiently, and save me from the expense of eating out night after night. Instead of coming home to face yet another job, I now can come home, not for more work, but to a leisurely, delicious meal that I can put together in a matter of minutes.

Meats that are already cooked and need only reheating are an easy way to do dinner in a hurry. Another fast way to put dinner together quickly is to choose a recipe that needs only a tossed salad or crunchy bread to complete the meal. Many of these recipes are in this category. Not one of the recipes in the section will take you more than 20 minutes to prepare. Not only that, but clean up time after the meal has also been reduced to a matter of minutes.

This main course cold platter needs no other accompaniment, however, it goes well after a hot soup or before a rich dessert.

COLD BEEF PLATTER

1 lb. waxy boiling potatoes

6 tablespoons creamy Italian-style dressing

1 lb. deli roast beef, cut in thick slices

3/4 lb. firm ripe tomatoes, cut in thick slices

1/4 cup minced parsley

1/4 cup minced chives

Place potatoes in a large pot of water; boil over medium-high heat until tender when pierced with a small knife. Drain and cool slightly. One at a time hold each potato under cold running water; slip off skin. Cut peeled potatoes into thick slices, arrange slices on a platter and sprinkle evenly with about 2 tablespoons of the dressing. Arrange beef over potatoes; sprinkle with 2 tablespoons of the dressing. Cover beef with tomato slices; top with remaining dressing. Scatter the parsley and chives over the top; serve at room temperature. Makes 4 servings.

Pick up salad bar vegetables and deli roast beef on your way home from work for this quick and delicious recipe.

DOUBLE QUICK BEEF LO MEIN

2 oz. Chinese vermicelli

1-1/2 tablespoons corn or other vegetable oil

1 teaspoon Oriental sesame oil

2 cups mixed raw "salad bar" vegetables about 1 lb. total weight: broccoli and cauliflower flowerets, green and red bell pepper strips, zucchini strips or slices, chopped green onion, etc.

1/4 cup water

1 small garlic clove, minced, or 1 teaspoon garlic juice

2 tablespoons soy sauce

2 tablespoons dry sherry

1/2 lb. lean very rare deli roast beef, cut into 1/4-inch strips

1/4 cup minced parsley

Place noodles in a large bowl; cover by about 2 inches with boiling water. Set aside. Heat corn and sesame oils in a large heavy skillet over medium heat. Add mixed vegetables; stir-fry about 1 minute. Add water; cover and steam about 2 minutes or until vegetables are crisp-tender. Add garlic, soy sauce and sherry. Stir to mix. Stir in beef; cook, lifting and stirring ingredients, until mixture is very hot. Drain and add noodles; toss to mix. Sprinkle with parsley. Makes 4 servings.

Here are actually two, not one, recipes. Though each could be served separately, they go so well together I find them hard to separate. For a total menu, serve them with tahine butter sandwiches and icy cold beer.

ROAST BEEF VINAIGRETTE & POTATO SALAD WITH CAPERS

8 thick rare roast beef slices from deli

About 2 tablespoons Dijon-style mustard

1 lb. fresh asparagus cooked until crisp-tender

1/4 cup Italian-style dressing with garlic

1 pint deli potato salad

1 tablespoon Dijon-style mustard

2 teaspoons prepared horseradish

1 tablespoon white wine vinegar

10 or 12 miniature pickled cocktail onions, drained

2 tablespoons capers, drained

1/2 cup chopped celery

Crisp lettuce leaves

2 plum tomatoes, each cut in 4 wedges

Ripe olives

One at a time, spread each slice of beef lightly with the 2 tablespoons of mustard; divide asparagus among slices and roll up. Place rolls in a shallow baking dish just large enough to hold them in 1 layer. Pour dressing over each, making sure that each roll is moistened thoroughly. Cover dish loosely with foil and let at stand at room temperature up to 1 hour before serving, or cover and seal dish with foil and refrigerate for several hours or until about 1/2 hour before serving. Place deli potato salad in a large bowl; add 1 tablespoon mustard, horseradish, vinegar, cocktail onions, capers and celery. Toss to mix ingredients. Let stand at room temperature until ready to serve, but no more than 1 hour, or cover bowl and refrigerate until about 1/2 hour before serving. Line a large platter with lettuce leaves and arrange beef rolls down center. Place mounds of potato salad around beef rolls. Garnish platter with tomato wedges and sprinkle paprika over beef rolls and salad. Or serve on individual plates. Makes 4 large or 8 small servings.

Variation
Substitute Kosher dill pickles for asparagus. Cut pickles lengthwise in quarters before rolling in beef slices.

A Mexican favorite, California style. Serve with blue corn chips for a special touch.

CHILI & AVOCADO SHELLS, CALIFORNIA STYLE

1 large ripe avocado	**1 pint ready-to-heat-and-eat chili, if possible buy freshly prepared chili from a Mexican restaurant**
1 teaspoon lemon juice	
1 tablespoon peanut oil or vegetable oil	**1 cup shredded lettuce, optional**
1 large Vidalia or other mild onion, chopped	**2 cups (1/2 lb.) shredded Monterey Jack cheese**
1 celery stalk, chopped	
1/2 small green bell pepper, chopped	**Tortilla chips, optional**
1 to 3 teaspoons chili powder	

Cut avocado in half, remove seeds and peel each half. Rub halves on all sides with lemon juice. Set aside. Pour oil into a large heavy skillet over medium heat. Add onion, celery and bell pepper. Cook, stirring, 2 to 3 minutes. Stir in chili powder (amount depends on how hot you like your chili). Add chili; cook, stirring, until bubbly hot. Cover 2 plates with shredded lettuce, if desired. Place an avocado half in the center of each. Top with chili mixture, dividing evenly and letting excess spill onto lettuce. Sprinkle each serving with cheese. If desired, serve with tortilla chips. Makes 2 servings.

Serving suggestions: For a Southwestern meal, serve this with corn chips, salsa and frosty mugs of beer. Choose Mexican pottery or pots of cactus to add an authentic touch.

If you think of creamed dried beef as a rather dull dish, try this version.

CREAMED BEEF ON TOMATO TOAST

4 thick firm ripe tomato slices

4 thick home style white bread slices

1 (2-1/2-oz.) jar dried beef

1/2 pint (1 cup) dairy sour cream

Sprinkling of white pepper

Dash of hot pepper sauce

Minced fresh or frozen chives

Preheat oven to 350F (175C). Place tomato slices on foil. Bake in preheated oven until hot, about 2 minutes. Lightly toast bread on each side. Place beef in a colander; rinse under cold water to rid it of some of the salty taste. Thoroughly blot dry; tear in thin shreds. Place shredded beef in top half of a double boiler over simmering water. Stir in sour cream; season with white pepper and hot pepper sauce. Cook, stirring often, until hot. To serve, place each toast slice on a plate; top with a hot tomato slice. Spoon beef mixture over each serving. Sprinkle with chives. Makes 4 servings.

Wow! Now this really is instant gourmet dining. You'll find the kebabs in the meat department at your favorite supermarket.

BEEF KEBABS WITH NEAR EASTERN RICE

1 cup long-grain Carolina or basmati rice, or 2 cups fully cooked leftover rice

2 fully cooked, commercially prepared, fresh, not frozen, beef kebabs on skewers with green bell pepper and onion, see page 13

1 tablespoon vegetable oil

1 tablespoon butter

1/2 cup raisins

1/2 cup slivered almonds

1/2 teaspoon curry powder

1/2 teaspoon Hungarian hot paprika

1 to 2 tablespoons minced fresh or frozen chives

1 to 2 teaspoons soy sauce or Worcestershire sauce

Preheat oven to 350F (175C). Line a baking sheet with foil. Cook rice following package directions or use leftover cooked rice. Set aside. Open package of kebabs and place them on foil-lined baking sheet. Bake in preheated oven about 10 minutes or until heated. Meanwhile, heat oil and butter in a large heavy skillet over medium heat. Stir in raisins, almonds, curry powder and paprika. Add rice and chives; stir until hot. Spoon rice onto 2 serving plates; top each with a heated kebab. Sprinkle with soy sauce. Makes 2 servings.

The secret in preparing this double-quick beef stew is in using fully cooked top round of beef.

EASY BEEF STEW

1 (3/4- to 1-lb.) pkg. fully cooked top round of beef (see page 13)

3 tablespoons butter

1 tablespoon corn oil or other vegetable oil

1 medium-size Vidalia or other mild onion, chopped

1 (14-1/2-oz.) can regular strength beef broth

1 lb. small new potatoes or red potatoes, peeled, cut in chunks

1/2 cup water

1 tablespoon all-purpose flour

1/2 to 1 teaspoon coarsely ground black pepper

1/2 teaspoon mixed Italian herbs

1 tablespoon thick steak sauce

Dash of hot pepper sauce

1 (12-oz.) jar extra-tiny Belgian carrots, drained

1 (12-1/4-oz.) jar small white boiled onions, drained

1/2 cup tiny frozen peas

Cut beef into bite-size cubes; set aside. In a large heavy skillet, heat butter and oil over medium heat. Add onion; cook, stirring, about 2 minutes or until limp. Add beef cubes and beef broth. Add potato chunks. Simmer mixture until potatoes are fork-tender. In a small bowl, combine water and flour; stir to a smooth paste. Scrape mixture into skillet; stir until liquid thickens slightly. Season with pepper and herbs. Stir in steak sauce and hot pepper sauce. Add carrots, onions and peas. Simmer stew, stirring occasionally, until hot. Makes 4 servings.

Frozen concentrated beef stock transforms this dish into a four-star French restaurant entree.

ROAST BEEF WITH SAUCE DIABLE

8 thick very rare roast beef slices from the deli

1 tablespoon butter

1/2 cup dry white wine

2 (2-oz.) containers frozen beef stock concentrate

1/2 teaspoon Worcestershire sauce

1/2 teaspoon Dijon-style mustard

1/8 teaspoon red (cayenne) pepper

Salt

2 tablespoons butter, room temperature

16 boiled new potatoes, optional

Bring roast beef to room temperature. Melt 1 tablespoon butter in a large heavy skillet over low heat. Add wine; boil until reduced to about 3 tablespoons. Add beef stock, stir until melted, then simmer 1 minute. Add Worcestershire sauce and mustard. Season with cayenne and salt. Remove skillet from heat; stir in remaining butter. One at a time, spear each slice of roast beef with a fork and dip it into the sauce. Place on 4 warm serving plates. Return skillet to heat and quickly bring sauce back to a brisk simmer. Divide sauce over each serving of meat. Serve, if desired, with boiled new potatoes. Makes 4 servings.

This is old-fashioned, down-home cooking at its best. Just like "mother used to make" but without the work and time she had to give to its making. Reserve remaining meat loaf for another use.

MUSTARD-GLAZED MEAT LOAF SLICES

6 (1/2-inch-thick) slices fresh, not frozen, fully cooked meat loaf

1 tablespoon brown sugar.

6 tablespoons Dijon-style or Creole-style mustard

6 fresh or canned pineapple slices

Preheat oven to 400F (205C). Line a baking sheet with foil. In a small bowl, combine sugar and mustard; stir to a smooth paste. Spread each meat loaf slice with mixture. Place slices on foil-lined baking sheet; surround with pineapple slices. Bake in preheated oven until hot and topping on meat loaf is glazed. Makes 2 or 3 servings.

For lovers of sauerkraut, here is a double-quick version of an old favorite.

SAUERKRAUT WITH POLISH SAUSAGE

1 (2-lb.) pkg. sauerkraut or 2 (1-lb.) cans sauerkraut

1/2 cup water

2 tablespoons hot and spicy ketchup

2 tablespoons corn or other vegetable oil

1 medium-size white onion, chopped

1 small green bell pepper, chopped

1 medium-size tart crisp apple, peeled, diced

1-1/2 lbs. Polish-type kielbasa (fully cooked Polish-type sausage), cut crosswise in 1/4-inch slices

Coarsely ground black pepper

Drain sauerkraut into a colander; rinse thoroughly under hot running water until water runs clear. Press out all possible water; set aside. Combine water and ketchup in a 1-cup measure, stir until smooth. Heat oil in a large heavy skillet over medium heat. Add onion, bell pepper and apple. Cook, stirring, 2 to 3 minutes or until onion is transparent. Add sausage, sauerkraut and ketchup mixture. Cook, stirring and lifting ingredients, until hot. Makes 6 servings.

Both the asparagus and the shrimp sauce can be prepared ahead and stored in the refrigerator until ready to use. If fresh asparagus are no longer available at your market, you can substitute crisp-cooked green beans or thick slices of sun-ripened tomatoes.

ASPARAGUS WITH HAM & SHRIMP SAUCE

1 tablespoon butter

1/2 lb. shrimp salad from deli

1 cup half and half

Salt and pepper

4 firm white bread slices, crusts removed

4 thin baked Virginia ham or Black Forest ham slices, room temperature

20 very thin asparagus spears or 16 medium-thick spears, crisp-cooked

Paprika

In top half of a double boiler, melt butter over medium heat. Stir in shrimp salad and half and half. Cook, stirring constantly, until hot. Season to taste with salt and pepper. Place over hot water and keep warm, stirring occasionally, until ready to use (up to 1/2 hour). Lightly toast bread on each side. Place each on a serving plate and top with a ham slice. Cover each with asparagus, spoon shrimp sauce over each. Sprinkle with paprika and serve at once. Makes 4 servings.

Tiny Swiss-style dumplings are tossed with Swiss cheese and ham slivers for this one-pot-easy-does-it supper dish.

SPAETZLE TOSS

1 (10-1/2-oz.) pkg. spaetzle

1 tablespoon butter

1 thin Westphalian ham slice, cut in small slivers

1/2 cup (2 oz.) shredded Swiss cheese

2 or 3 small radishes, chopped

1/2 cup half and half or whipping cream

Salt and pepper

Cook spaetzle following package directions; drain into a colander. Melt butter in a large heavy skillet over medium heat. Add ham; stir 1 minute. Stir in cooked spaetzle, cheese, radishes and half and half. Season lightly with salt and pepper. Cook, stirring and tossing ingredients, until hot. Makes 4 to 6 servings.

A hearty yet light version of an old fashioned favorite. The meat is lean and non-greasy, the cabbage is cooked only until crisp-tender and the potatoes are steamed.

CORNED BEEF & CABBAGE WITH POTATOES

4 small steamed new potatoes, about 1/2 lb. total weight

1 small green cabbage, about 1 lb. total weight

1 to 2 tablespoons soft butter

1/2 cup water

Salt and pepper

4 medium-thick deli corned beef slices, about 1/2 lb. total weight

Deli rye bread, optional

Set potatoes aside; bring to room temperature, if cooked ahead. Remove and discard loose outer leaves from cabbage; cut cabbage lengthwise into 4 wedges. With a small sharp knife, remove almost all of tough core at root end, leaving only enough to hold wedges together. Spread 1 side of each wedge with the soft butter, dividing evenly. Place wedges, butter side up, in a single layer in a large heavy skillet and pour water around them. Sprinkle lightly with salt and pepper. Loosely roll each slice of corned beef and place them between cabbage wedges. Cut each cooked potato into 4 wedges and place over corned beef and cabbage. Cover; cook over medium-high heat only until cabbage is crisp-tender and meat and potatoes are hot. Serve, if desired, with deli rye and butter. Makes 4 servings.

Serving suggestions: Serve this for an easy St. Patrick's Day dinner. Add buttered rye bread and imported beer or stout. End the meal with Chocolate, Chocolate, Chocolate Cake, page 157.

SEAFOOD

Simply superb fish dishes not only can but must be prepared in true instant gourmet fashion—quickly. Fish and shellfish should not be overcooked—even a minute or two longer than is necessary will result in lack of flavor and changes in texture and taste. Many hot seafood dishes must be eaten as soon as they are ready—they are not keep-in-the-oven-until-served fare. Others can be kept at room temperature up to 30 minutes or even a little longer. Please, please don't put them in the refrigerator, then attempt to reheat them. The results can be disastrous.

For the no-time-to-cook cook, extra help is at hand. You can now buy fresh or frozen peeled, deveined and cooked shrimp; cooked lobster; canned, fresh or frozen crabmeat; imitation crabmeat, double-quick cooking scallops; and shucked fresh oysters, as well as canned salmon and tuna, and last but not least, individually frozen fish fillets that need not be thawed before cooking.

As I'm sure you know, modern nutritionists tell us seafood is not only healthful but great diet fare and should be eaten often. We do, but that's not why we eat it. It's quick and easy to prepare, but we eat it simply because it tastes grand and to our way of thinking there's no better reason.

Though the method of cooking is like an Oriental stir-fry, the result is more like a French stew. Double-quick cooking is the secret to its fresh taste.

SEAFOOD STIR-FRY WITH TOMATOES

Brushettes with Aioli Sauce, see recipe opposite, optional

2 tablespoons corn oil or other vegetable oil

1 lb. large scallops, drained, cut horizontally in half

1 lb. medium shrimp, shelled, deveined

1/2 lb. imitation crabmeat

4 small zucchini, thinly sliced

2 celery stalks, diagonally cut in 1/2-inch slices

1 (19-oz.) can imported Italian plum tomatoes

1 to 2 teaspoons virgin olive oil or avocado oil

1 tablespoon lime juice

Salt and pepper

BRUSHETTES WITH AIOLI SAUCE, OPTIONAL

12 thick crusty French bread slices

About 1 tablespoon olive oil

1/2 cup mayonnaise

2 or 3 dashes garlic juice

Make Brushettes, if desired. Heat corn oil in a very large heavy skillet over medium heat. Add scallops and shrimp; cook, stirring, 2 to 3 minutes, or until scallops are firm and shrimp are pink. Stir in crabmeat, zucchini and celery. Drain tomatoes; reserve 1/2 cup juice. Add tomatoes and reserved tomato juice. With the tip of a spatula, break tomatoes into small chunks; cook, stirring, until ingredients are hot. Stir in olive oil and lime juice; season to taste with salt and pepper. Ladle mixture into shallow soup bowls or rimmed plates. If desired, serve with Brushette. Makes 4 to 6 servings.

BRUSHETTE WITH AIOLI SAUCE

Preheat broiler. Lightly brush each bread slice on both sides with olive oil. Place on a baking sheet. Broil, turning once, until lightly browned. In a small bowl, combine mayonnaise and garlic juice; beat with fork until blended. Spread on grilled bread slices. Let stand at room temperature until ready to serve. If desired, just before serving place in pre-heated oven until warmed. Makes 12 servings.

An adaptation, of course, but slightly exotic nonetheless and wonderfully good.

MALAYAN STIR-FRY

1/2 cup water

2 teaspoons cornstarch

Dash of garlic juice

1 cup half and half

1 tablespoon peanut oil or vegetable oil

1/4 lb. green bell pepper strips from salad bar or 1 medium-size green bell pepper, cut in narrow strips

1/4 lb. chopped onion from salad bar or 1 medium-size onion, chopped

1/4 cup water

3/4 lb. fresh sole fillet or 1 (12-oz.) pkg. individually frozen sole fillets, thawed

1 (10-1/2-oz.) can pineapple tidbits, drained

2 oz. slivered almonds

1 (4-oz.) jar pimento strips, drained

1 tablespoon soy sauce

2 to 3 cups hot cooked rice, or reheated leftover rice

Soy sauce to taste

Toasted coconut flakes, optional

In a small bowl, combine 1/2 cup water, cornstarch and garlic. Stir in half and half; set aside. Heat oil in a large heavy skillet or wok over medium heat. Add pepper and onion; stir-fry about 1 minute or until onion is limp. Add remaining 1/4 cup water; bring to a boil. Arrange fish over vegetable mixture. Cover; steam about 2 minutes or until fish turns from translucent to opaque. Uncover, break fish into large chunks with tip of a spatula; add pineapple, almonds and pimentos. Toss to mix. Stir cornstarch mixture; add cornstarch mixture and 1 tablespoon soy sauce. Cook, stirring, until hot. Serve over hot rice; sprinkle servings with additional soy sauce to taste. If desired, sprinkle with toasted coconut. Makes 4 servings.

One pot does it all—deliciously.

PASTA CON PESCO

1 teaspoon corn oil or other vegetable oil

1/4 teaspoon salt

1 (8-oz.) pkg. linguine

1/4 lb. butter, room temperature

1 medium-size tomato, halved, seeded, chopped

1/4 lb. large mushrooms, diced

6 to 8 imitation crabmeat legs

Salt and pepper

Fill a large pot with water; bring to a boil. Stir in oil and salt. Add linguine, stirring once to separate strands. Cook until tender yet still firm to the bite. Drain into a colander leaving about 1/2 cup of the water in the pot. Return pot to medium heat and add butter; stir until butter has melted and starchy water and butter form a light creamy sauce. Stir in tomato, mushrooms and crabmeat. Add pasta; cook, stirring and lifting ingredients, until well mixed and hot. If desired, season with additional salt and pepper. Makes 4 servings.

Here's another incredible three-ingredient recipe! Serve with sautéed zucchini strips.

SCALLOPS IN SALSA CREAM SAUCE

1 lb. large scallops, cut crosswise into thick slices

3/4 mild or hot salsa

1/4 cup half and half

Salt, optional

Rinse scallops in a colander under cold running water; blot dry on paper towels. Arrange in a single layer in a steamer over simmering water. Cover; let steam until scallops are opaque, about 2 minutes. Set aside. Combine salsa and half and half in a large, heavy saucepan over medium heat. Cook, stirring occasionally, until hot. Add steamed scallops; cook 1 minute. Season with salt, if desired. Makes 2 large servings.

Variation
Sauté scallops in 3 tablespoons vegetable oil in a large skillet over medium-high heat until opaque, about 2 minutes. Drain on paper towels before adding to sauce.

Fresh salmon steaks can range in color from blood red to bright orange or delicate pink, and vary slightly in size, color, cost and taste. Buy whichever is fresh and available in your particular market. No matter which you select, this recipe will give you a colorful entree. The cooking method gives you moist, but not overcooked, fish.

SALMON CAESAR EN PAPILLOTE

1/2 cup thick and creamy Caesar salad dressing

4 salmon steaks, about 6 oz. each

1 medium-size zucchini, cut lengthwise into strips

6 to 8 small pitted Niçoise olives, sliced

Preheat oven to 400F (205C). Cut 4 (12-inch-square) foil pieces. Pour salad dressing into a shallow dish. Dip each salmon steak on both sides in salad dressing; hold briefly over dressing to drain slightly. Place each on a foil sheet. Place zucchini strips over salmon. Top with remaining salad dressing. Sprinkle with olive slices. Bring sides of foil pieces up toward center; seal tightly, leaving sufficient room for steaming. Place sealed packets on a baking sheet. Bake in preheated oven 18 minutes. Remove from oven; let stand 5 minutes. Slash foil packets with a knife; carefully pull back foil. With a spatula, lift salmon with vegetables onto serving plates. Serve hot. Makes 4 servings.

Olive spread is an Italian import of minced ripe olives and herbs.

PASTA WITH TUNA & OLIVE SPREAD

1 (1-lb.) jar pasta sauce with chunky vegetables

1 to 2 dashes garlic juice, optional

1/4 cup olive spread (olivata)

1 (3-1/2-oz.) can solid pack white tuna, drained, broken into chunks

Freshly ground pepper

1 teaspoon vegetable oil

1 (1-lb.) pkg. linguine or other long thin pasta strands, such as fusilli

Grated Parmesan cheese, optional

In a medium-size saucepan, combine pasta sauce and, if desired, garlic juice. Bring to a simmer. Stir in olive spread and tuna. Sprinkle lightly with pepper; set aside. Bring a large pot of water to a full boil; stir in oil. Add linguine; stir once to separate strands. Cook until tender yet firm to the bite. Drain into a colander; return pasta to pot and add sauce mixture. Toss to mix; if desired, sprinkle each servings with Parmesan cheese. Makes 6 servings.

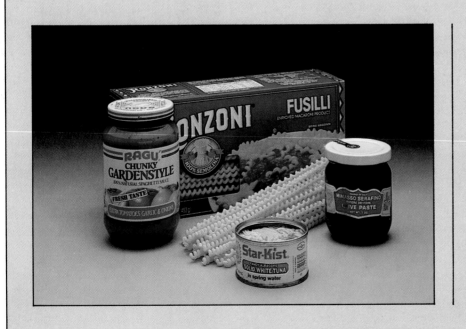

Serving suggestions: For a quick party, make the peperonata on page 46 for the appetizer, then for dessert serve Fresh Fruit in Asti Spumante, page 152. Serve a light red Italian wine with the pasta and finish the meal with expresso.

This is an elegant and flavorful light luncheon or supper dish.

COLD POACHED SALMON WITH BLUE CHEESE MAYONNAISE

Blue Cheese Mayonnaise, see below

1 (2-oz.) container frozen fish and lobster stock concentrate

2 tablespoons lemon juice

1-1/2 cups water

4 (3/4- to 1-inch-thick) salmon steaks

1/4 teaspoon dry herbs de Provençe

1/4 teaspoon salt

1 pint deli potato salad

Thick tomato slices

Pitted olives or small crisp pickles

BLUE CHEESE MAYONNAISE

1/4 cup (1 oz.) crumbled blue cheese, room temperature

1 cup mayonnaise

1 tablespoon capers, drained

1 teaspoon lemon juice

1 tablespoon minced parsley, optional

Prepare Blue Cheese Mayonnaise; refrigerate until ready to use. Heat frozen stock in a large saucepan over low heat until melted. Add lemon juice and water; bring to a brisk simmer. Add salmon steaks in a single layer (if necessary, add additional water to cover steaks completely). Add herbs. Let simmer until fish turns from translucent to opaque, about 15 minutes. Remove saucepan from heat; let steaks cool in broth to room temperature. Transfer steaks to a shallow baking dish, cover with cooking stock and refrigerate until ready to use, up to 8 hours. Remove each steak from the stock with a spatula, drain briefly over pan, then transfer each to 1 side of a serving plate. Top each with about 1 tablespoon of the mayonnaise (serve remaining mayonnaise separately). Arrange potato salad, tomato slices and olives to each plate. Makes 4 servings.

BLUE CHEESE MAYONNAISE
Combine ingredients in a medium-size bowl; stir to mix. Refrigerate until ready to use.

For this recipe we have used individually frozen sole fillets for two reasons: they don't have to be thawed and they bake in less than 12 minutes.

BAKED SOLE WITH PESTO MAYONNAISE

2 tablespoons butter

1 (12-oz.) pkg. individually frozen sole fillets

2 tablespoons pesto sauce

1/2 cup mayonnaise

1 teaspoon lemon juice

1 or 2 dashes garlic juice, optional

1/2 teaspoon salt

Paprika

Preheat oven to 400F (205C). Melt butter in a square 8-inch baking dish. Remove from heat; add fillets, turning each to coat with butter. Bake, uncovered, in preheated oven 8 to 10 minutes or until fish turns from translucent to opaque. While fish are baking, place remaining ingredients in a small bowl; beat until smooth. Spoon over fish; bake 2 to 3 minutes, or until topping is hot and lightly flecked with brown. Makes 4 servings.

Ripe olives and capers lend a taste of Provençe to this simple yet seductive dish.

FILLET OF SOLE WITH VEGETABLES PROVENÇAL

2 medium-size tomatoes, seeded, cut into narrow strips

2 small cucumbers, peeled, seeded, diced

1 tablespoon lemon juice

1 teaspoon salt

1/4 teaspoon dry Herbs de Provençe

1/4 cup butter

1 (7-oz.) can whole kernel corn, drained

12 pitted ripe olives, sliced

2 tablespoons capers, drained

1 (12-oz.) pkg. individually frozen sole fillets or other firm white fish, or 4 fresh sole fillets, about 12 ounces total weight

About 2 tablespoons minced parsley or sprinkling of imported Hungarian paprika

Place tomatoes and cucumber in a large bowl. Sprinkle with lemon juice, salt and herbs. Toss to mix. Melt butter in a large heavy skillet over medium heat. Add vegetable mixture; cook, stirring frequently, until hot. Arrange fish fillets over vegetable mixture; cover and steam until fish turns from translucent to opaque, 4 to 6 minutes. Transfer each fillet to a large serving plate and surround with vegetable mixture. Sprinkle fish with minced parsley or paprika. Serve at once. Makes 4 servings.

You can serve these delicious salmon steaks as either a hot or cold entree.

POACHED SALMON STEAKS WITH SALSA

1 cup Salsa, see opposite	**1/4 cup lemon juice**
2-1/2 cups water	**SALSA**
1/2 cup dry vermouth or white wine	**3/4 cup mild or hot salsa**
1/4 cup lemon juice	**2 tablespoons lemon juice**
2 teaspoons salt	
4 (about 1/2-inch thick) salmon steaks about 1-1/2 lbs. total weight	

Prepare Salsa; set aside. In a large skillet over high heat, bring water, vermouth, lemon juice and salt to a brisk simmer. Add salmon steaks. Cover; simmer 6 to 8 minutes or until salmon turns from translucent to opaque. With a slotted spatula, transfer each steak to a serving plate or place steaks in a single layer in storage container, cover and refrigerate until chilled or ready to serve. Serve warm or chilled with Salsa. Makes 4 servings.

Salsa:
Pour salsa into a small bowl; stir in lemon juice. Serve at room temperature or refrigerate until chilled.

Serving suggestions: Hot or cold, this is a satisfying entree. Accompany with steamed new potatoes and crisp-tender vegetables. For wine aficionados try one of the California Chardonnays.

An adaptation of a famous recipe from Virginia's hunt country.

BAKED OYSTER, TURKEY & HAM CASSEROLE

1/4 lb. butter

2 cups seasoned bread crumb stuffing mix

1 pint medium-size oysters and their liquid

1 thick slice (about 4 oz.) deli turkey white meat, chopped

1 thick slice (about 4 oz.) deli baked Virginia ham, chopped

Paprika

Preheat oven to 375F (190C). Melt butter in a large heavy skillet over low heat; stir in stuffing mix and liquid from oysters. Spoon half of mixture into a long shallow (9" x 6") baking dish. Top with oysters, turkey and ham. Cover with remaining dressing mix; sprinkle with paprika. The casserole may be prepared ahead, covered and stored in refrigerator for several hours. However, it should be removed from the refrigerator about 1/2 hour before baking. Bake in preheated oven 12 to 15 minutes or until hot. Serve at once. Makes 4 servings.

This recipe proves once again that splendid pasta sauces don't demand hours to prepare.

LINGUINE WITH FRESH TOMATO SAUCE

2 teaspoons light and fruity olive oil

3 large or 4 medium-size firm, ripe tomatoes, peeled, seeded, diced

1/2 teaspoon mixed Italian herbs

1/4 teaspoon salt

1/2 teaspoon freshly ground black pepper

1/2 teaspoon corn oil or other vegetable oil

1/4 teaspoon salt

1 (8-oz.) pkg. linguine

Preheat oven to 375F (190C). Cover a large baking sheet with foil; brush with 1 teaspoon of the olive oil. Add tomatoes; sprinkle evenly with herbs, salt and pepper. Drizzle with the remaining olive oil. Bake in preheated oven 4 to 5 minutes. Set aside. Fill a large pot with water; bring to full boil over high heat. Stir in corn oil and salt. Add linguine; stir once, then cook until tender yet firm to the bite. Drain into a colander, leaving about 2 tablespoons of water in the bottom of the pot. Place pot over medium-low heat; add baked tomatoes and drained linguine; toss to mix ingredients thoroughly. Serve at once. Make 2 large or 4 medium-size servings.

Variation
For a heartier dish, add a small can of drained and flaked tuna or salmon to the pasta along with the tomatoes or, if you like, as we do, a small can of drained and chopped anchovy fillets or caper-stuffed anchovy fillets.

POULTRY

Though almost all poultry is relatively easy to prepare, when time is of the essence it's a real joy to leave that chore to someone else. Especially now when there is truly delicious as well as nourishing fully cooked turkey, chicken and even duck available at our markets, ready to bring home and eat "as is" or to use in preparing elegant entrees that can be brought to the table in a matter of minutes. When planning a menu, remember easy dishes using already prepared poultry products. For a easy Sunday brunch, serve Chicken Almond Hash, page 90, with fresh fruit and hot poppy seed rolls from the bakery. Add miniature Danish from a pastry shop and lots of good coffee for a relaxing meal.

Having a patio dinner? Serve sliced smoked turkey breast with cranberry sauce laced with prepared horseradish. Add a selection of deli salads and several kinds of hearty breads. Choose a quick dessert to complete the meal.

For a holiday meal without hassle, order a roasted turkey with all the trimmmings from a local restaurant. Add a quick soup, such as French Onion Soup, page 64, some vegetables and perhaps one of the liqueur-soaked cakes for dessert. You still have to do the dishes, but the cooking is already done!

But these are only a few possibilities for menus. Look over the recipes in this section—we think you'll like them and find many ways to use them in your own menus.

Buy the roasted duck from a Chinese restaurant or the deli department of your supermarket. You can either buy the cooked rice from the same Chinese restaurant or you can use leftover cooked rice from your refrigerator.

ROAST DUCK WITH TAHINI SAUCE & RICE

1 (2- to 3-lb.) roasted duck

3 tablespoons tahini paste

3 tablespoons soy sauce

3 tablespoons water

2 teaspoons rice vinegar

1 teaspoon hot chili oil

1/4 teaspoon garlic juice

1 cup cold cooked rice

Preheat oven to 400F (205C). Cut duck lengthwise into halves or have the Chinese restaurant or deli do this for you. In a medium-size bowl, combine tahini paste, soy sauce, water, vinegar, chili oil and garlic juice; stir to mix. Line a baking sheet with foil. With a pastry brush or your fingers, coat each duck half on all sides with some of the tahini mixture. Place on foil-lined baking sheet. Place rice in a heatproof bowl; stir in about half of the remaining tahini mixture. Pour the rest of tahini mixture into a small heatproof bowl. Place duck on bottom rack of oven; place rice and sauce on second rack. Bake until heated. Transfer 1 duck half and half the rice to each of 2 serving plates. Place heated sauce in bowl on a small plate; serve separately. Makes 2 servings.

Variation
Rotisserie broiled or roasted chicken can be substituted for the duck.

Served with a mixed green salad with vinaigrette dressing, this makes an extremely pleasurable meal—a tray of fresh strawberries with small bowls of warm honey to dip them in would make an elegant dessert.

CHICKEN CURRY

1 tablespoon vegetable oil

2 tablespoons butter

1 small onion, chopped

3 celery stalks, chopped

1 (12-oz.) jar curry sauce

2 pickled peach halves in heavy syrup, drained, chopped

2 tablespoons heavy syrup from pickled peaches

1/2 lb. cooked chicken or turkey breast, cut in small dice

About 2 cups packaged croutons

1/4 cup minced parsley

Heat oil and butter in a large heavy skillet over medium heat. Add onion and celery; cook, stirring, about 2 minutes or until vegetables have softened. Add curry sauce, peaches and peach juice. Stir in chicken. Cook, stirring, until hot. Divide croutons among 4 serving plates. Spoon curry over croutons; sprinkle with minced parsley. Makes 4 servings.

Buy the chicken on your way home from work or wherever. Preferably select one that is still warm from the rotisserie heat, still moist and only lightly browned.

SWEET & SOUR CHICKEN

1 (3-1/2- to 4-lb.) rotisserie broiled chicken

1/4 cup honey

1/4 cup Dijon-style mustard

2 tablespoons butter

1 teaspoon soy sauce

Line a broiler pan with foil. Split broiled chicken in half lengthwise; place halves, skin side up, on broiler rack over foil lined broiler pan. Preheat oven to 400F (205C). Combine remaining ingredients in the top half of a double boiler over simmering water. Stir until blended and warm. With a pastry brush or your fingers (messy but effective), spread mixture evenly over skin side of each chicken half. Bake in preheated oven 5 to 8 minutes, or until skin is lightly glazed. While chicken is baking, replace remaining glaze over simmering water. Transfer each broiler half to a warm serving plate; serve at once. Pour warm glaze into 2 small Oriental-style dipping bowls or 1 larger bowl and serve with chicken. Makes 2 servings.

Serve, if you like, with hot cooked rice and mango chutney. For extra fast preparation, buy fresh vegetables, chopped and ready to cook, from your supermarket salad bar.

HUNGARIAN CHICKEN

1 tablespoon corn or other vegetable oil

1 tablespoon butter

1 large onion, chopped

1 large green bell pepper, chopped

1 teaspoon hot Hungarian paprika

1 (14-oz.) can plum tomatoes

1 lb. raw chicken nuggets, each cut crosswise in 1/4-inch slices

1/4 lb. mushrooms, chopped

2 teaspoons Worcestershire sauce

1 tablespoon lemon juice

Salt and pepper

1 tablespoon cornstarch

3 tablespoons water

1 cup half and half

Heat oil and butter in a large heavy skillet over low heat. Add onion and bell pepper. Cook, stirring, about 5 minutes or until vegetables are limp. Stir in paprika; add tomatoes and their juice. With a tip of a spatula, break tomatoes into small chunks. Add chicken, mushrooms, Worcestershire sauce and lemon juice. Season lightly with salt and pepper. Cover and cook about 10 minutes, stirring occasionally. In a small bowl, combine cornstarch, water and half and half. Add chicken mixture. Cook, stirring, until liquid thickens and mixture is hot. Makes 4 servings.

Curry powder lends a slight Middle Eastern flavor to this savory dish.

CHICKEN ALMOND HASH

1/2 cup half and half	**4 thin baked Virginia ham slices**
1/2 teaspoon curry powder	**4 firm white bread slices**
1 pint deli chicken salad	**Imported Hungarian paprika, optional**
1 (2-oz) pkg. slivered almonds	

Preheat oven to 350F (175C). Line a baking sheet with foil. In top half of double boiler, combine half and half and curry powder; cook over simmering water, stirring until smooth. Stir in chicken salad and almonds. Keep warm over hot water. Place ham slices on foil-lined baking sheet in preheated oven until hot. Lightly toast bread slices; place each on a serving plate. Place a slice of ham on each slice of toast. Top with hot chicken salad mixture, dividing evenly. Sprinkle with paprika and serve at once. Makes 4 servings.

Serving suggestions: Fresh fruit and lemonade make this a complete Spring luncheon. If your guests have a sweet tooth, serve one of the easy ice cream dishes from the desserts chapter.

Because wheat noodles do not need to be cooked, this authentic Oriental entree can be prepared all in one skillet.

CHICKEN LO MEIN

2 to 3 oz. Chinese vermicelli

1 (16-oz.) pkg. frozen mixed Oriental-style vegetables without seasoning

3/4 lb. raw chicken nuggets

1-1/2 tablespoons corn or other vegetable oil

1 teaspoon Oriental sesame oil

1/4 cup water

1 tablespoon soy sauce

2 tablespoons dry sherry

1 teaspoon garlic juice

2 to 3 tablespoons coarsely chopped cilantro

3 tablespoons chopped cashews

1/4 cup minced chives or green onions

1 (3-oz.) can crisp Chinese noodles, optional

Soy sauce, optional

Place vermicelli in a large bowl; cover by about 2 inches with boiling water. Set aside. Unwrap and place frozen vegetables on a large plate until partially thawed, about 5 minutes. Rinse chicken; pat dry. Cut each chicken piece lengthwise into about 1/4-inch strips. Pour corn oil and sesame oil into a large heavy skillet over medium-high heat. Add chicken; cook, stirring, until no longer pink, about 2 minutes. Add partially thawed vegetables; cook, stirring, about 1 minute. Pour in water, cover and let steam about 4 to 5 minutes, or until vegetables are crisp-tender. Drain noodles and add to skillet, lift and stir to mix with vegetables and chicken. Add 1 table-spoon soy sauce, sherry and garlic. Cook, stirring, about 1 minute longer. Stir in cilantro, cashews and chives. Transfer mixture to 4 serving plates or large shallow soup bowls, dividing evenly. Sprinkle each serving with crisp noodles and additional soy sauce, if desired. Makes 4 servings.

A combination hot and cold salad that's differently delicious.

CHUNKY CHICKEN SALAD

2 cups shredded Romaine lettuce or other lettuce

1 tomato, halved, seeded, cut in narrow strips

1/2 small green bell pepper, minced

1/2 cup thinly sliced celery

1/4 cup chopped crisp pickles

2 to 3 tablespoons Russian dressing or other thick creamy prepared dressing

1 to 2 teaspoons lemon juice

Salt to taste

1 (10-oz.) pkg. frozen chicken nuggets

Preheat oven as directed on package of chicken nuggets. Combine vegetables with dressing, lemon juice and salt; toss to mix. Refrigerate while baking chicken nuggets. Bake nuggets as directed on package. Ladle cold salad mixture onto serving plates. Top each serving with hot chicken nuggets and serve at once. Makes 2 large or 4 small salads.

For authentic curry, the accompaniments are as important as the dish itself. In India, when that country was under British rule, curry was served with pomp and circumstance. Each accompaniment was served by a different serving boy, so it was called "Five Boy," "Seven Boy," or however many accompaniments were used, each served in an individual bowl and passed at the table.

SEVEN-BOY CURRIED CHICKEN & SHRIMP

1/4 lb. butter

1 tablespoon curry powder

3 tablespoons all-purpose flour

2 cups milk

2 cups chicken broth

2 tablespoons dry sherry

2 cups diced cooked chicken or turkey

1 (6-oz.) pkg. tiny frozen shrimp, thawed

Hot cooked rice or Oriental noodles

Accompaniments: Major Grey's chutney, finely chopped salted peanuts, shredded coconut, tart jelly, finely chopped sweet pickles, chopped ripe olives, sliced pimento-stuffed green olives, seedless raisins

Melt butter in a large heavy skillet over low heat. Stir in curry powder and flour; cook until bubbly. Slowly stir in milk and broth. Bring to a simmer; cook, stirring, until smooth. Add sherry, chicken and shrimp. Continue to stir until mixture is hot. Serve over hot rice or noodles. Pass accompaniments at the table. Makes 6 to 8 servings.

In this recipe we have made use of commercially prepared frozen chicken stock concentrate. The result is a very rich sauce that is nonetheless low calorie.

CHICKEN BREAST WITH SAUCE SUPREME

3/4 to 1 lb. skinned, boned chicken breast pieces, flattened

1/4 cup lemon juice

1/4 cup water

1 to 2 dashes garlic juice, optional

2 (2-oz.) containers frozen chicken stock concentrate

Salt and pepper

3/4 cup half and half

2 tablespoons minced fresh or frozen chives

Place chicken pieces in a large deep skillet over low heat. Pour in lemon juice and water; add garlic juice, if desired. Bring to a simmer; cook chicken until firm and white, about 5 minutes. Remove chicken from liquid; set aside. Pour off liquid from skillet, wipe clean with paper towels, then return to medium heat. Add stock; stir until melted. Increase heat to high, season with salt and pepper, and cook 2 to 3 minutes, stirring, until liquid has reduced slightly. Remove skillet from heat; stir in half and half. Add chicken, return skillet to low heat and cook, stirring, until chicken is hot. Sprinkle with chives. Makes 4 servings.

It will take you no more than 5 minutes to prepare the ingredients for this elegant dish.

CHICKEN HASH WITH OYSTERS, VIRGINIA STYLE

1 (1-lb.) can Italian-style whole plum tomatoes

1 small onion, chopped

1/2 small green bell pepper, chopped

1 (8-oz.) can whole kernel corn, drained

1 (8-oz.) can lima beans, drained

1/2 lb. chicken breast from deli, cut in small cubes

1 thick Virginia ham slice, about 1/4 lb., diced

1 tablespoon minced frozen or fresh chives

2 or 3 dashes hot pepper sauce

Salt and pepper

2 tablespoons butter

1 tablespoon corn or vegetable oil

1/2 pint medium or large oysters, drained

2 cups hot cooked rice or leftover rice, reheated

Pour about 1 tablespoon of the tomato juice from canned tomatoes into a large mixing bowl. Discard remaining juice. Add tomatoes to bowl, breaking them up with your fingers into small pieces as they are added. Add onion and bell pepper. Stir in corn, beans, chicken, ham, chives and hot pepper sauce. Season lightly with salt and pepper. Heat butter and oil in a large heavy skillet over medium heat. Add the vegetable mixture; stir until hot. Place oysters on top; cover pan and cook 4 to 5 minutes or until edges of oysters curl. Stir oysters down into vegetable mixture. Serve over hot rice. Makes 4 servings.

When you see the word Florentine on a French menu, it simply means made with spinach. Our double easy and quick version makes use of frozen chopped spinach.

SMOKED TURKEY FLORENTINE

2 (10-oz.) pkgs. frozen chopped spinach

1 (12-oz.) jar hollandaise sauce

1/2 lb. thinly sliced smoked turkey breast

Paprika

8 firm white bread slices, lightly toasted

Preheat oven to 375F (190C). Place frozen spinach in a colander; hold under hot running water, breaking up frozen blocks with your hands, until completely thawed. Squeeze out all possible water and transfer to a large bowl. Stir in about 1/3 of the hollandaise sauce. Spread mixture evenly in a long shallow 9" x 6" baking dish. Cover with overlapping slices of turkey; top with remaining hollandaise sauce. Sprinkle evenly with paprika. Bake in preheated oven about 10 minutes or until hot. Place 1 slice of toast on each of 4 serving plates; top with turkey mixture. Serve with remaining toast slices. Makes 4 servings.

The perfect light luncheon and supper dish. It can be prepared ahead then baked just before serving.

INDIVIDUAL HAM, TURKEY & ASPARAGUS CASSEROLES WITH CHEESE

3 heaping tablespoons bernaise sauce, about 1/3 of 9.3 oz. jar

4 baked Virginia ham slices, about 1/4 lb. total weight

4 smoked turkey breast slices, about 1/4 lb. total weight

4 imported Swiss Emmenthaler or Gruyère cheese slices, about 1/4 lb. total weight

12 medium-size or 16 very thin, fresh asparagus spears, cooked, or 1 (16-oz.) can white asparagus tips

8 thick center slices ripe tomato (2 medium-size tomatoes)

Paprika

Preheat oven to 350F (175C). Lightly butter the bottom and sides of 4 individual (7" x 3") oval gratin dishes. Spread the bottom of each with about 1 teaspoon of the bernaise sauce. Cut ham, turkey and cheese into slices the size of dishes; cut leftover scraps into narrow 1/2-inch strips. Place a ham slice in the bottom of each dish. Spread very lightly with a little of the bernaise sauce. Place 4 or 6 asparagus spears over each ham slice. Cover each with a turkey slice and spread, again lightly, with sauce. Arrange 2 tomato slices over each turkey slice; surround each with the turkey, ham and cheese strips. Top each casserole with remaining bernaise sauce; smooth out evenly. Cover each with a cheese slice and sprinkle with paprika. Bake casseroles in pre-heated oven about 10 minutes or until cheese has melted and sauce has bubbled up around edge of dishes. Let stand about 5 minutes before serving. Makes 4 servings.

As with all short order cooking, the instant gourmet need only be reminded to have every ingredient measured and ready to use before the actual cooking begins.

TURKEY HASH DELUXE

2 egg yolks

1/2 teaspoon garlic juice, optional

1/2 cup half and half

3 tablespoons butter

1/2 small Vidalia onion, minced

1/2 small green bell pepper, chopped

1/2 lb. smoked turkey breast, cut in small dice

1/4 cup chopped ripe olives

1/4 cup chicken broth

Salt and pepper

4 baked puff pastry shells or 4 thick firm white bread slices, toasted

Place egg yolks in a small bowl; beat until blended. If desired, stir in garlic juice. Add half and half; beat until smooth. Set aside. Melt butter in a large heavy skillet over low heat. Stir in onion and bell pepper. Cook, stirring, about 2 minutes or until softened. Stir in turkey and olives; add broth and season lightly with salt and pepper. Stir until turkey is thoroughly heated. Add egg yolk mixture; continue to stir until liquid thickens (do not allow to boil). Spoon hash into puff pastry shells or over toasted bread; serve immediately. Makes 4 servings.

Here's another recipe about liberation—from the kitchen. It takes less than 15 minutes to prepare.

SMOKED TURKEY WITH PINEAPPLE

3/4 lb. smoked turkey	1 (5-1/2-oz.) can pineapple tidbits
3/4 cup water	1 (2-oz.) pkg. cashew nuts, coarsely chopped
2 tablespoons dry sherry	2 teaspoons cornstarch
1 tablespoon honey	1/4 cup water
1 small bell pepper, cut in strips	2 teaspoons white wine vinegar
1 medium onion, chopped	1 tablespoon soy sauce
1/4 cup chopped crystalized ginger	2 cups cold cooked rice or 3 cups loosely packed shredded Napa cabbage

Cut turkey in 1/4-inch-thick slices; cut slices crosswise in 1/4-inch-thick strips. Place turkey, 3/4 cup water, sherry and honey in a wok or large heavy skillet over medium heat. Stir until liquid comes to a full boil; reduce heat. Simmer until water has reduced by about half. Stir in bell pepper and onion; simmer 1 minute. Add ginger, pineapple with juice and cashews. In a 1-cup measure, combine cornstarch with 1/4 cup water, vinegar and soy sauce. Stir to blend; add to turkey mixture. Stir until liquid thickens slightly. Add cold cooked rice or shredded cabbage. Lift and stir ingredients until hot. Makes 6 servings.

Variation
Do not add rice or cabbage. Spoon rice or cabbage onto a serving plate. Top with chicken mixture.

Serving suggestions: Start the meal with takeout egg rolls and finish with fresh fruit and jasmine tea.

DINNERS ON A PLATE

I especially like those meals that I call "Dinners on a Plate." Not only are they made with such good-for-you things as fresh vegetables, nutritious meats, fish, shellfish and poultry, they taste postively delicious! My own favorites include Sizzling Steak with Onion Rings & Green Beans and Chicken Cordon Bleu. My friends are surprised and delighted by these meals. I think you will also enjoy them.

Anyone of these complete main courses requires less time to bring to the table than it does to heat and serve a TV dinner, even in a microwave oven! All you'll need to prepare each serving is a heatproof dinner plate and heatproof plate mats to protect your dining table. There are no serving bowls to wash, everything is cooked and served on the same plate.

What an attractive dinner this makes—and it's delicious, too!

FLOUNDER WITH GREEN PEAS & BROILED TOMATO

For each serving:

1 tablespoon butter

Salt

1/3 (10-oz.) pkg. frozen green peas

2 thick tomato slices

1 teaspoon sugar

2 individually frozen flounder fillets

2 teaspoons mayonnaise

1 teaspoon minced green onion or chives

Place butter in a small heatproof bowl in cold oven. Set oven temperature at 400F (205C). As soon as butter has melted, remove bowl from oven and stir in a little salt. Place frozen peas in a medium-size bowl; cover by about 1 inch with boiling water. Let stand about 30 seconds; drain and place on 1 side of a large heatproof serving plate. Drizzle with a little of the melted butter. Place tomato slices next to peas; sprinkle with sugar and drizzle with a little of the melted butter. Place frozen fish on other side of plate; drizzle with remaining butter. Turn fish, butter side down; spread top with mayonnaise. Sprinkle evenly with green onion. Bake in preheated oven 12 to 15 minutes, or until fish turns from translucent to opaque. Serve immediately. Makes 1 serving.

The potatoes for this colorful entree can be prepared two or three hours ahead after which the plate can be assembled and baked in a matter of minutes.

SALMON WITH BROCCOLI, CAULIFLOWER & DICED POTATOES

For each serving:

1 tablespoon butter

2 small cooked new potatoes, chopped

Light sprinkling of chili powder, about 1/4 teaspoon

1 (2-1/2- to 3-inch-thick) salmon fillet, about 1/3 pound

3 or 4 broccoli flowerets, broken in small pieces

3 or 4 cauliflowerets, broken in small pieces

1 tablespoons lemon juice

1 tablespoon capers

1 teaspoon juice from capers

Butter slivers, about 1 teaspoon

Salt and coarsely ground black pepper

Place butter in a small heatproof bowl in cold oven. Set oven temperature at 400F (205C). As soon as butter has melted, remove from oven. Add potatoes and chili powder; toss to mix. Using a small sharp knife, cut salmon at a 45-degree angle into the thinnest possible slices; set aside. Place potatoes and vegetables on 1 side of heatproof dinner plate; bake in oven about 5 minutes or until hot. Remove plate from oven and arrange salmon slices on other side of plate; sprinkle with lemon juice, capers and caper juice. Top vegetables with slivers of butter; season lightly with salt and pepper. Bake 2 minutes or until salmon slices are firm. Makes 1 serving.

This is an easy Oriental-style dinner for two!

JUMBO SHRIMP WITH ORIENTAL RICE

8 or 12 jumbo shrimp

1/4 cup Oriental sweet and sour sauce

1 tablespoon soy sauce

1 tablespoon lemon juice

1 teaspoon vegetable oil

1 or 2 drops Oriental sesame oil

1 (8-oz.) pkg. frozen Chinese pea pods, thawed

4 or 6 canned water chestnuts, drained, chopped

1-1/2 cups cold cooked rice

1 tablespoon soy sauce

1 or 2 drops Oriental sesame oil

1 tablespoon raisins, optional

Soy sauce to taste

Peel and devein shrimp, leaving tail section attached. In a medium-size bowl, combine sweet and sour sauce, 1 tablespoon soy sauce, lemon juice, vegetable oil and 1 or 2 drops sesame oil. Add shrimp; let stand at room temperature 10 to 15 minutes. Preheat oven to 400F (205C). In another bowl, combine pea pods, water chestnuts, rice, 1 tablespoon soy sauce and 1 or 2 drops sesame oil and raisins, if desired; toss to mix. Drain shrimp over bowl; place 4 to 6 on each of 2 heatproof plates. Place rice mixture on other side of each plate, dividing evenly. Drizzle any remaining sweet and sour sauce mixture over shrimp. Bake in preheated oven until shrimp are firm and pink and rice mixture hot, about 8 minutes. Serve at once. Makes 2 servings.

A very pretty and flavorful dish to set before the king, queen or your favorite person.

SCALLOPS FLORENTINE

1 tablespoon butter

1 (10-oz.) pkg. frozen chopped spinach

1 to 2 teaspoons lemon juice

Salt and pepper

1 pint bay or sea scallops

2 tablespoons whipping cream

1 teaspoon tomato paste

1 tablespoon grated Parmesan cheese

Pitted ripe olives, optional, cut into slivers

Place butter in a small heatproof bowl in cold oven. Set oven temperature at 400F (205C). Set aside. Place frozen spinach in a colander; hold under hot running water, breaking up block as it thaws. When completely thawed, squeeze out all possible water and transfer to medium-size bowl. Stir in melted butter and lemon juice. Season lightly with salt and pepper. Mound mixture on 2 large heatproof dinner plates, dividing evenly. Spread out each spinach mound into a circle; press edges up to form a small rim. Leave bay scallops whole; cut sea scallops into quarters. Place in a medium-size bowl; stir in remaining ingredients. Place mixture in the center of each mound of spinach, dividing evenly. Bake in preheated oven until spinach mixture is hot and scallops are opaque through center, about 5 minutes. If desired, sprinkle each serving with olive slivers. Makes 2 servings.

For this recipe, lean pork fillet (tenderloin) is sliced paper thin so that it is cooked thoroughly yet still moist and flavorful.

ORIENTAL PORK WITH PEAS & NOODLES

1 (1/2- to 3/4-lb.) pork tenderloin

1 tablespoon honey

1 teaspoon Dijon-style mustard

2 tablespoons orange juice

1 teaspoon soy sauce

3 to 4 oz. Oriental vermicelli

1 (10-oz.) pkg. frozen Chinese pea pods, thawed

Minced fresh parsley or chives

Soy sauce to taste

Place pork in the freezer until firm but not frozen. With a sharp knife, cut pork at a 45-degree angle into very thin slices; place in a medium-size bowl. Stir in honey, mustard, orange juice and 1 teaspoon soy sauce; toss to mix. Let stand about 15 minutes. Place noodles in a medium-size bowl; cover by about 2 inches with boiling water. Let stand until softened, about 15 minutes. Drain and reserve marinade from pork; set pork aside. Preheat oven to 400F (205C). Place pork slices slightly overlapping on 1 side of 2 heatproof dinner plates. Bake in preheated oven about 5 minutes. Drain noodles; place on other side of each plate; drizzle with remaining marinade and top with peas. Return plates to oven; bake 2 to 3 minutes or until pork is no longer pink. Makes 2 servings.

You don't have to be Southern to enjoy!

SOUTHERN HAM & SWEET POTATOES WITH MIXED VEGETABLES

4 (1/4-inch-thick) fully cooked or packaged ham slices

1 tablespoon orange marmalade

1 (1-lb.) can sweet potatoes, drained

1 to 2 teaspoons lemon juice

1 teaspoon sugar

Salt

1 large or 2 small yellow (summer) squash, diced

1 medium or 2 small zucchini, diced

4 medium-size cherry tomatoes, halved

1 tablespoon cold butter, cut in slivers

Pepper

Preheat oven to 400F (205C). Spread each ham slice lightly with marmalade; place slightly overlapping on each of 2 heatproof dinner plates. Place sweet potatoes on other side of plates; sprinkle lightly with lemon juice, sugar and salt. Combine squash and tomatoes; add to plates. Dot with butter; season with salt and pepper. Bake in preheated oven 10 minutes or until vegetables are crisp-tender. Makes 2 servings.

A "down-home" style menu featuring fried chicken, slaw stuffed tomatoes and baked beans. If you have the tomato at home, all you need do is pick up the remaining component parts of the menu at the take-out window of your favorite fast food chicken restaurant.

SOUTHERN FRIED CHICKEN ON A PLATE

1 medium to large tomato

Salt

4 large pieces fried chicken—2 breast halves, 2 thighs—from takeout chicken restaurant

1 teaspoon Dijon-style mustard or similar mustard

2 teaspoons orange marmalade

1/2 pint or 2 portion-size containers cole slaw

1 teaspoon drained prepared horseradish, optional

Paprika, optional

1/2 pint or 2 portion-size containers baked beans

1/2 cup well-drained canned pineapple tidbits

Preheat oven to 400F (205C). Cut tomato in half. With a small spoon, scoop out and discard all seeds and center pulp. Sprinkle cavities lightly with salt; place cut side down on paper towels to drain while preparing remaining ingredients. One at a time, use a small knife and your fingers to loosen and pull out bones from each piece of chicken. Place boned chicken on a flat surface and flatten slightly. Using knife, slit skin on 1 side and pull it away from meat, leaving other side attached to meat. With knife, make a few small slits in meat and spread entire surface with a small amount of the mustard and marmalade. Fold skin back over meat. Place 1 breast and 1 thigh on each of 2 heatproof dinner

plates. Drain all possible liquid from cole slaw and, if desired, stir in horseradish. Stuff tomato shells with mixture, dividing evenly. Press slaw mixture firmly into shells and, if desired, sprinkle each with paprika. Place 1 filled shell on each serving plate. Drain almost all liquid from beans; stir in pineapple tidbits. Place on serving plates, dividing evenly. Bake in preheated oven 8 to 10 minutes; serve at once. Makes 2 servings.

Can takeout fried chicken be elegant? Yes, it can—here's proof.

BREAST OF CHICKEN WITH ZUCCHINI & BRANDIED PEACHES

3 large breasts of fried chicken from takeout chicken restaurant

2 medium or 3 small zucchini

2 brandied peach halves

Grated Parmesan cheese, about 1 teaspoon

4 lemon wedges

Preheat oven to 400F (205C). One at a time, use a small knife and your fingers to loosen and pull all bones from each chicken breast. Place boned chicken breasts on a cutting board; cut each lengthwise into 1/4-inch strips. Place strips slightly overlapping on 1 side of each of 2 heatproof dinner plates, dividing evenly. Trim ends from zucchini, cut lengthwise into long, thin strips. Place strips in center of plates, dividing evenly. Arrange peach halves on other side of plates. Bake in preheated oven 8 to 10 minutes. Remove from oven; sprinkle zucchini strips with grated cheese. Add lemon wedges to each plate; serve at once. Makes 2 servings.

Our quick version of this classic way of preparing chicken is as delicious as the original recipe.

CHICKEN CORDON BLEU

For each serving:

1 tablespoon butter

2 large boneless chicken breast halves, about 3 oz. total weight

Salt

About 1 teaspoon Dijon-style mustard

2 thin proscuitto, Westphalian ham or other ham slices

2 thick Swiss cheese slices, cut in 1/2-inch strips

1 large tomato, seeded, coarsely chopped

2 or 3 small broccoli flowerets, coarsely chopped

1 celery stalk, chopped

1/2 (8-oz.) can whole-kernel corn, drained

Place butter in a small heatproof bowl in cold oven. Set oven temperature at 400F (205C). As soon as butter is melted, remove from oven and set aside. Place chicken between wax paper sheets; pound evenly until no more than about 1/4-inch thick. Sprinkle lightly with salt and spread with mustard. Trim ham slices so that they fit chicken pieces, leaving a 1/4-inch border. Place a ham slice over each chicken, top with 1/2 of the cheese strips. Roll up chicken; place on a heatproof plate. Sprinkle lightly with salt; top with remaining cheese strips. In a medium-size bowl, combine tomato, broccoli, celery, corn and melted butter; toss to mix. Season lightly with salt. Arrange vegetables on other side of plate. Bake in preheated oven 8 to 10 minutes or until chicken is firm and white through center. Makes 1 serving.

As with all of these dinners on a plate, this one is perfect when you want Chinese-style food, especially when dining alone.

CHICKEN WITH ORIENTAL VEGETABLES

For each serving:

1 tablespoon soy sauce

1 green onion, minced

1 tablespoon water-packed ginger root slices, drained, chopped

3 drops Oriental sesame oil

1 drop hot pepper sauce

1/3 (8-oz.) pkg. Chinese pea pods

4 or 5 canned straw mushrooms, drained, rinsed

3 ears canned baby corn, rinsed

3 radishes, coarsely chopped

1/4 chicken breast, skinned, boned, cut diagonally in 1/4-inch strips

Preheat oven to 400F (205C). In a medium-size bowl, combine all ingredients; toss to coat well. Place mixture on a heatproof plate. Bake in preheated oven until vegetables are crisp-tender and chicken strips firm and white through center, 8 to 10 minutes. Serve immediately. Makes 1 serving.

When you don't have time to prepare it, but want something highly flavorful like Tex-Mex food, this just might be the answer.

CHILI BEEF WITH BEANS

1 (1-lb.) can cannellini (white) beans

1/2 lb. lean ground beef

1/4 cup chopped onion from salad bar or 1 small onion, chopped

1/4 cup chopped green bell pepper from salad bar or 1/2 small green bell pepper, chopped

1/4 cup chopped celery from salad bar or 1 celery stalk, chopped

2 tablespoons chili sauce or hot and spicy ketchup

1 to 2 teaspoons chili powder

1/4 teaspoon salt

Coarsely ground black pepper

Preheat oven to 400F (205C). Drain beans in a colander; rinse under cold running water until water runs clear, about 30 seconds. Place in a large bowl; add remaining ingredients and toss to mix thoroughly. Place on 2 heatproof plates, dividing evenly. Bake in preheated oven until hot, about 8 minutes. Makes 2 servings.

Variation
Use 2 thick very rare roast beef slices from deli instead of ground beef. Cut beef into small cubes. Combine cubes and any juice from the beef and rinsed beans in a medium bowl. Add remaining ingredients and proceed as above.

This is an easy way to use leftover potatoes.

BEEF FILLET WITH ZUCCHINI & NEW POTATOES

For each serving:

1 thick (3- to 3-1/2-oz.) beef fillet

1 small zucchini

2 cold boiled new potatoes, brought to room temperature

Salt and coarsely ground pepper

Worcestershire sauce

1 tablespoon butter, cut in slivers

Paprika

Preheat oven to 400F (205C). Holding a very sharp knife so that the blade is almost parallel to the work surface, cut beef crosswise into thin slices. Place slices on 1 side of a heatproof dinner plate. Trim and cut zucchini at a 45-degree angle into thin oval slices; place on other side of plate. Peel and cut potatoes into small cubes; add to plate. Sprinkle beef, zucchini and potato lightly with salt. Sprinkle beef with pepper and Worcestershire sauce. Top zucchini and potato with butter. Sprinkle paprika over potatoes. Bake in preheated oven 3 to 4 minutes, or until beef is medium rare. Makes 1 serving.

Because the steak is thinly sliced it cooks in only minutes!

SIZZLING STEAK WITH ONION RINGS & GREEN BEANS

For each serving:

1 thick (3-1/2- to 4-oz.) beef fillet

2 tablespoons butter

Light sprinkling of salt

1/3 (10-oz.) pkg. frozen French-cut green beans

3 or 4 thick slices Vidalia or red onion

1 tablespoon thick steak sauce

Crusty rolls, optional

Holding a very sharp knife so that the blade is almost parallel to the work surface, cut steak crosswise in thin slices; set aside. Place butter in a small heat-proof bowl in cold oven. Set oven temperature at 400F (205C). As soon as butter has melted, remove it from oven and add a sprinkling of salt. Place frozen beans in a medium-size bowl; cover by about 1 inch with boiling water. Let stand about 30 seconds; drain and place on 1 side of a large heatproof serving plate. Drizzle with a little of the melted butter. Dip each onion slice in melted butter; hold over bowl to drain slightly. Arrange slices next to beans. Bake in preheated oven 2 minutes. Add steak slices to other side of plate; drizzle with remaining butter. Bake 3 to 4 minutes. Spoon steak sauce over beef slices and bake 1 minute or until steak is to desired doneness. If desired, serve with crusty rolls. Makes 1 serving.

EGGS & CHEESE

Eggs and cheese are probably the most versatile of all foods: they fit into every menu, from an early breakfast to a late night supper. Home from work, too tired to eat out, almost too weary to cook and the cupboard is almost bare? With a few eggs in the refrigerator and a bit of cheese plus a little of "this and that," you can cook up a pleasant little meal in a matter of minutes, one that is neither too heavy nor too light, a meal that can restore your energy and lift your spirits.

Consider the following recipes—all are quick, easy and almost effortless to prepare. There's also a bonus: good as these recipes are, each also has many possible variations. Not only can the ingredients be adapted to your taste, they can also be adapted to what's on hand in your kitchen. For example, when preparing the Baked Vegetable Frittata Cake, you can substitute yellow squash for the zucchini, chopped celery for the green or red bell pepper and any grated cheese you have on hand for the Parmesan. When preparing the Eggnog & Croissant French Toast, try brandy or sherry in place of the rum, and instead of the maple syrup you can substitute any syrup or jelly in your refrigerator. For the Glorified Scrambled Eggs, deviled ham can replace Smithfield ham spread for buttering the bread. And, of course, when preparing the Double-Quick Eggs Florentine, any type of cheese can be used for the topping.

The point here is that these recipes can be prepared as written or used as takeoff points for your own inspirational cooking. It's part of the fun of being an instant gourmet.

A great way to end a "night on the town."

ENGLISH EGG MUFFINS

2 English muffins, split

1 tablespoon butter

1 small Vidalia onion, chopped

4 large eggs

1/3 cup half and half

Salt and pepper

2 tablespoons butter

4 thick (about 1/4 lb.) Cheddar cheese slices

Place broiler rack about 4 inches from heat source; preheat broiler to high. Place muffin halves on a baking sheet; broil until lightly toasted. Spread muffins with 1 tablespoon butter; set aside on baking sheet. In a medium-size bowl, combine onion, eggs and half and half. Beat with whisk until blended; season lightly with salt and pepper. Melt remaining butter in a large heavy skillet over low heat. Add egg mixture; cook, stirring occasionally, only until eggs are set but still moist. Spoon onto muffin halves; top with cheese and place under preheated broiler just until cheese begins to melt. Makes 2 servings.

Basically this is a sweet omelet, thickened with a little flour and baked in the oven. It's not a new recipe, far from it, but has recently become newly popular.

FRESH BERRY PUFF

2 tablespoons unsalted butter, room temperature

2 large eggs

1/3 cup milk

2 tablespoons brandy or rum

1/2 cup all-purpose flour

1/4 cup packed light brown sugar

1 cup coarsely chopped strawberries, whole raspberries, blackberries or blueberries

2 tablespoons powdered sugar

Preheat oven to 450F (230C). Coat bottom and sides of a heavy 9- or 10-inch skillet with the butter. Place eggs, milk, brandy, flour and brown sugar in work bowl of food processor; process until well mixed. Or place these ingredients in a large bowl and beat with whisk until well blended. Pour mixture into buttered skillet; top with berries. Bake in preheated oven until well puffed and the surface is very lightly browned, about 15 minutes. Sprinkle with powdered sugar and serve immediately. Makes 2 servings.

This puffy, crisp, part omelet, part soufflé tastes great with a crisp salad or bowl of hot soup.

OMELET SOUFFLÉ

2 tablespoons unsalted butter

1/2 cup milk

1/2 cup sifted all-purpose flour

3 eggs

1/4 cup grated Parmesan cheese

1/4 teaspoon salt

Pepper

Preheat oven to 475F (245C). Melt butter in a heavy 9- or 10-inch skillet over medium heat; set aside. Place remaining ingredients in order given in work bowl of food processor or blender; process until well mixed and frothy. Add all but about 1/2 teaspoon of melted butter from skillet; blend briefly. Pour mixture back into skillet; bake in preheated oven until surface is browned and crusty, 10 to 12 minutes. Serve from skillet. Makes 2 to 3 servings.

Home from a hard day's work and your emergency shelf is almost bare? Serve these special scrambled eggs.

GLORIFIED SCRAMBLED EGGS

2 home-style white bread slices

2 teaspoons Smithfield ham spread

2 tablespoons butter

4 eggs

1/2 cup low-fat cottage cheese

1 tablespoon minced chives

Salt

Freshly ground black pepper

Imported hot Hungarian paprika

Lightly toast bread slices; spread with ham spread. Place on warmed serving plates. Melt butter in a heavy skillet over medium heat until bubbly. Remove skillet from heat, break in eggs and beat with a fork until blended. Stir in cottage cheese, chives and salt. Return skillet to low heat; cook, stirring constantly, until very lightly scrambled. Spoon onto prepared toast slices; sprinkle with pepper and paprika. Makes 2 servings.

This classic omelet never goes out of style.

EGGS JARDINIERE

4 thick bacon slices

2 tablespoons butter

1 small Vidalia onion, chopped

6 eggs

Salt and coarsely ground black pepper

4 slices (about 1/4 lb.) mild or sharp Cheddar cheese

Cook bacon in a 10-inch skillet over low heat. When crisp, remove from skillet and drain on paper towels; crumble when cool. Pour bacon fat from skillet and discard; add butter and onion. Cook, stirring, until onion is limp, about 2 minutes. Add eggs to skillet; sprinkle lightly with salt and heavily with pepper. Stir once and then cook until the bottom of the omelet begins to set, lifting edges with spatula to allow uncooked egg to run underneath. When the surface of the omelet is almost firm, remove skillet from heat and top with crumbled bacon. Cover bacon with cheese slices. Broil about 4 inches from heat just until cheese begins to melt. Cut into wedges to serve. Makes 4 servings.

Not only do eggs prepared in this manner make for a very colorful and elegant breakfast or brunch-time entree, there's this bonus: they can be prepared several hours or even overnight before you plan to bake and serve them.

DOUBLE-QUICK EGGS FLORENTINE

2 (10-oz.) pkgs. frozen chopped spinach

1 tablespoon mayonnaise

2 or 3 dashes hot pepper sauce

1/4 teaspoon salt

1/4 teaspoon pepper

4 large or jumbo eggs

4 thin slices (about 1/4 lb.) mozzarella cheese

Preheat oven to 375F (190C). Place frozen blocks of spinach in a colander and hold under cold running water; as it thaws, use your hands to break up large frozen chunks as the blocks begin to separate. Pick thawed spinach up in your hands and squeeze out all possible liquid. Transfer to a medium-size bowl; stir in mayonnaise, hot pepper sauce, salt and pepper. Lightly butter 4 individual size (7" x 5") baking dishes. Fill each with spinach mixture, spreading mixture over entire dish. Then, with the back of a large spoon, make a slight indentation in the center of each and break in 1 egg. If necessary, trim cheese slices to fit into top of each dish. Place 1 slice over egg and spinach mixture in each dish. (If desired, cover dish with foil; refrigerate until about 20 minutes before baking. Can be prepared several hours ahead or overnight. Remove foil before baking.) Place baking dishes on flat tray in preheated oven 10 to 15 minutes or until cheese has melted and eggs have set. Making 4 servings.

The perfect answer for a festive brunch anytime during the holiday season.

EGGNOG & CROISSANT FRENCH TOAST

6 large thick croissants, 1 day old

2 cups commercially prepared eggnog

2 tablespoons light rum

1/2 cup unsalted butter

2 tablespoons sugar mixed with 1 teaspoon ground cinnamon

Maple syrup, optional

Cut each croissant lengthwise into 2 halves. In a medium-size bowl, combine eggnog and rum; beat with whisk to blend. Dip each croissant half into mixture, turning to coat both sides. Melt 2 tablespoons of the butter in a large heavy skillet over medium-high heat. Add 2 or 3 of the croissant halves; fry until golden on both sides. Repeat with remaining halves and butter. Sprinkle with cinnamon-sugar mixture. Serve with maple syrup, if desired. Makes 6 servings.

Serving suggestions: Perfect for brunch—accompany with fresh fruit and coffee. For a festive occasion, add champagne for a meal about which your guests will rave.

Wintertime and the cooking is easy—with this savory puffed, oven-baked omelet.

BAKED VEGETABLE FRITTATA

2 tablespoons unsalted butter, room temperature

1 tablespoon peanut or vegetable oil

1 small onion, chopped

1 small zucchini, chopped

1/2 cup chopped green or red bell pepper

2 eggs

1/2 cup milk

1-1/4 cups all-purpose flour

1/4 cup grated Parmesan cheese

2 or 3 dashes hot pepper sauce

Dash of Worcestershire sauce

Salt and pepper

Preheat oven to 450F (230C). Heat butter and oil in a large heavy skillet over medium heat; add onion, zucchini and bell pepper. Cook, stirring, until vegetables are crisp-tender, about 2 minutes. Remove skillet from heat. In a medium-size bowl, combine eggs, milk, flour, cheese and seasonings; beat with whisk until well blended. Pour over vegetables in the skillet and immediately place skillet in preheated oven. Bake until puffed and golden, about 15 minutes. Serve at once. Makes 2 servings.

This classic sauce glorifies many different entrees, but is especially flavorful with baked eggs.

BAKED EGGS WITH BLACK BUTTER CAPER SAUCE

4 thin, firm white bread slices, crust removed

2 large or jumbo eggs

Salt and pepper

2 tablespoons butter

1 teaspoon white wine vinegar

1 tablespoon small capers, drained

Preheat oven to 375F (190C). Lightly toast bread slices; place 1 slice on each of 2 serving plates. Cut remaining slices diagonally into triangles. Lightly butter 2 (1-cup) custard cups. Break 1 egg into each; sprinkle lightly with salt and pepper. Cover each dish tightly with foil. Place dishes on a baking sheet. Bake in preheated oven until whites are firm and yolks are set but are still slightly soft, about 10 minutes. Run a small knife around edge of each baking dish to loosen eggs. Unmold each onto a slice of the toast. Heat butter in a small skillet over medium heat until melted and just beginning to brown. Reduce heat slightly, then stir in vinegar and capers. Cook, stirring, about 1 minute, then immediately pour over baked eggs on toast, dividing evenly. Add 2 toast triangles to each plate; serve at once. Makes 2 servings.

SANDWICHES

The number of possible sandwich creations an inventive gourmet can dream up is beyond count. To start, one needs only two slices of bread and a slice of deli cheese or meat. Considering that there are at least 100 different cheeses and prepared meats at the deli department of your supermarket or gourmet food shop, at least 1000 different sandwich variations are immediately possible. Then consider the different kinds of breads: crusty French- or Italian-style loaves, fat round loaves of sourdough, pumpernickel or deli rye, croissants and pita breads, as well as thin-sliced white or whole wheat—and how many more?

With this simple combination of bread and meat or cheese you can go on to grilled sandwiches, sandwiches that are broiled and open-faced sandwiches, both hot and cold.

Now start adding other filling ingredients: crisp pickles, chopped olives, sliced avocados or tomatoes or crisp-cooked bacon, then add mustard, mayonnaise, Russian dressing or vinaigrette and the possible variations can be multiplied seemingly without end.

Pizza, America's favorite Italian import, is actually an open-faced sandwich on flat yeast bread. For a quick and easy, yet delicious base, you can substitute Italian Boboli or focaccia bread, then top it with commercially prepared tomato sauce, meat, cheeses, olives, anchovies, or just about any other ingredient you want to add, from smoked salmon to caviar.

Though the original definition, dreamed up by the Earl of Sandwich was that of an easy meal of meat and bread that could be eaten without interrupting his card game, a sandwich today is often served as a main course luncheon dish or light supper to be eaten with knife and fork, or it can be a massive hero or hoagie that requires your total attention. With or without soup or a salad, a sandwich can indeed be a glorious meal. The Earl himself would be astonished to know what great and glorious fare that is now attributed to his name.

Another version of a classic sandwich.

CROQUES MONSIEUR RIVIERA STYLE

1/2 cup (2 oz.) coarsely grated Gruyère cheese

1/2 cup whipping cream

Salt and pepper

8 or 10 thin firm white bread slices

1/4 lb. very thinly sliced Westphalian or Black Forest ham

1/2 cup unsalted butter

In a medium-size bowl, combine cheese and cream; stir to a thick paste. Add salt and pepper to taste. Cut crust from bread (reserve for other use); spread each slice with cheese mixture. Place ham slices on half the bread slices; trim ham to fit. Cover with remaining bread slices; press down lightly. Cut in half diagonally. Melt half the butter in a large heavy skillet over medium heat. Add half of the sandwiches; fry, turning once, until crisp and lightly browned. Drain on paper towels. Add remaining butter and fry remaining sandwiches. Serve hot. Makes 4 or 5 sandwiches.

The tapenade makes this simple turkey sandwich into one that is very special indeed.

ROAST TURKEY SANDWICH WITH TAPENADE

3 tablespoons imported olive spread (olivata)

1 teaspoon anchovy paste

1 teaspoon lemon juice

1 teaspoon Dijon-style mustard

Coarsely ground black pepper

4 deli rye bread slices from center of loaf

6 or 8 thin deli roast turkey breast slices

Cherry tomatoes

Dill pickle slices

In a medium-size bowl, combine olive spread and anchovy paste. Stir in lemon juice and mustard; season lightly with pepper. Spread each bread slice with mixture. Top 2 slices with turkey, top with remaining bread slices and cut each sandwich diagonally in half. Serve with cherry tomatoes and pickle slices. Makes 2 sandwiches.

The excellence of this sandwich depends on really great deli rye bread.

REUBEN SANDWICH

For each sandwich:

2 deli rye bread slices

2 tablespoons Russian dressing

2 thin Swiss cheese slices

2 thin deli corned beef slices

1/2 cup sauerkraut, well drained

1 tablespoon mayonnaise

Kosher dill pickle, optional

Spread both slices of bread on 1 side with some of dressing. Top 1 slice with cheese and corned beef; cover with sauerkraut and remaining dressing. Cover with remaining bread, dressing side in. Spread outside of sandwich with mayonnaise. Heat a large heavy skillet over medium-high heat. When hot, add sandwich; press down until bottom slice of bread is lightly browned; turn and brown other side. Cut sandwich in half and, if desired, serve with pickle. Makes 1 sandwich.

This sandwich is part Welsh rarebit, part Swiss fondue. It's a great early or late, late supper dish.

CRÔUTE A FROMAGE

2 tablespoons butter, room temperature

4 home-style white bread slices

1 egg yolk

1 cup (4 oz.) shredded Swiss cheese or Gruyère cheese

1 tablespoon half and half or water

Salt and pepper

1 egg white

Preheat broiler. Butter each bread slice on 1 side. Place, buttered side up, on a baking sheet. Broil until lightly toasted on buttered side only. Set aside. Beat egg yolk in a small bowl with a fork until light and lemony in color. Fold in cheese and half and half. Season lightly with salt and pepper. In a separate bowl, beat egg white until soft peaks form. Fold in cheese mixture. Place bread slices, toasted side up, on baking sheet. Top with cheese mixture. Broil 5 to 6 inches from heat until puffed and golden. Makes 2 or 4 servings.

This knife and fork sandwich makes a TV dinner worth eating.

WELSH RAREBIT SANDWICH

1 (10-oz.) pkg. frozen chopped broccoli

1/2 cup mayonnaise

2 tablespoons all-purpose flour

1 teaspoon Dijon-style mustard

2 or 3 dashes Worcestershire sauce

3/4 cup beer

2 cups (8-oz.) shredded mild Cheddar cheese

8 whole wheat bread slices, toasted, halved diagonally

3 large tomatoes, cut in thick slices

Place broccoli in colander; rinse under hot water until thawed. Set aside. In a large saucepan, stir together mayonnaise, flour, mustard and Worcestershire sauce. Cook over medium heat, stirring, about 1 minute; gradually stir in beer. Cook, stirring constantly, until thick (do not allow to boil). Add cheese; cook and stir until melted. Stir in broccoli; cook, stirring, until hot. Arrange toast and tomato slices alternately on 4 plates. Pour sauce over each serving. Serve at once. Makes 4 servings.

Smoked turkey is included here instead of the usual ham.

GRILLED CHEESE SANDWICH ON DELI RYE

For each sandwich:

2 thin deli light rye bread slices

1 teaspoon unsalted butter, room temperature

1 Gruyère cheese slice

About 1 tablespoon deli cole slaw, thoroughly drained

1 smoked turkey breast slice

Spread 1 slice of bread with about 1/2 of the butter; cover with cheese slice. Spread cole slaw evenly over cheese; cover with turkey slice and remaining bread. Press sandwich down lightly and spread remaining butter onto each side of bread. Heat a large heavy skillet over high heat. When hot, add sandwich; press down lightly until grilled on 1 side. Turn and grill on second side. Cut sandwich diagonally in half; serve at once. Makes 1 sandwich.

A sublime coupling of ham and creamy Brie cheese in one sumptuous sandwich.

FRENCH-STYLE HERO SANDWICH

1/4 cup unsalted butter, room temperature

1 tablespoon Dijon-style mustard

1 long loaf French-style bread

6 thin baked ham slices

6 thin French Brie cheese slices

1 medium-size firm ripe tomato, seeded, cut in narrow strips

1 medium-size cucumber, peeled, seeded, diced

In a small bowl, combine butter and mustard. Split loaf of bread horizontally; spread cut surfaces with mustard mixture. Layer ham and cheese on 1 side of bread; top with tomato and cucumber. Cover with remaining bread. Press down lightly; cut crosswise into 4 thick slices. Makes 4 sandwiches.

This is a grilled cheese sandwich deluxe!

HOT CROISSANT WITH AVOCADO & CHEDDAR CHEESE

For each sandwich:

1 large croissant

About 1 teaspoon Dijon-style mustard

About 1 teaspoon butter, room temperature

1/2 small avocado, chopped

About 1 oz. shredded or chopped mild or sharp Cheddar cheese

Deli carrot salad, optional

Preheat oven to 350F (175C). Split croissant from rounded side, leaving ends attached. Force open slightly and spread each inside with mustard and butter; fill with avocado and cheese. Place on a baking sheet. Bake in preheated oven only until heated and cheese begins to melt. If desired, serve with deli salad. Makes 1 sandwich.

You can, if you like, serve this sandwich with lightly chilled champagne. And why not? You deserve it.

RICH BOY SANDWICH

1 (8-oz.) pkg. cream cheese, room temperature	**Small cherry tomatoes**
2 tablespoons half and half	**Cornichon pickles**
1 to 2 dashes garlic juice, optional	**Sprigs of watercress briefly dipped in vinaigrette dressing**
1 oz. red salmon caviar or lumpfish caviar	**Green ripe olives**
4 large croissants	**Niçoise olives**

Preheat oven to 450F (230C). In a small bowl, combine cream cheese, half and half and, if desired, garlic juice. Beat with a fork until well blended. Gently stir in caviar. Cut a deep lengthwise pocket in inner side of each croissant. Stuff pockets with cheese mixture, dividing evenly. Wrap each in foil; place on a baking sheet. Bake in preheated oven about 10 minutes. Place sandwiches on individual plates; garnish with tomatoes, pickles, watercress and olives. Serve at once. Makes 4 servings.

Serving suggestions: This is a great way to "stretch" caviar, yet add an extravagant feel to a lunch. Use your best china and silver, and serve by the pool for an elegant meal.

Here is a sumptuous variation to the traditional toasted cheese sandwich.

GRILLED HAM & SAGA CHEESE WITH MUSHROOMS

For each sandwich:

1 firm white bread slice

1 thin deli baked ham slice

1 firm ripe tomato slice

1 oz. crumbled or chopped saga blue cheese with mushrooms

1 thin Swiss cheese slice

Sliced pimento-stuffed olives, optional

Preheat broiler. Lightly toast bread on 1 side. Cover with ham slice and tomato slice, sprinkle with blue cheese and cover with Swiss cheese slice. Place on a baking sheet. Broil until cheeses have softened and are beginning to melt. If desired, top with sliced olives. Makes 1 sandwich.

This sandwich makes a delicious light supper.

HOT MUSHROOM & HAM SANDWICH

1/2 cup butter

1/2 lb. large fresh mushrooms, sliced

1 tablespoon all-purpose flour

1-1/2 cups milk

2 tablespoons half and half

1/2 cup slivered ham

Salt and pepper

4 thick home-style white bread slices, lightly toasted

Paprika, optional

Melt butter in a large heavy skillet over medium heat; stir in mushrooms. Cook, stirring occasionally, until slightly softened, about 5 minutes; stir in flour. Cook, stirring, until bubbly; slowly stir in milk. Cook, stirring constantly, until mixture thickens. Add half and half and ham slivers; cook, stirring, until hot. Season to taste with salt and pepper. Place each slice of toast on a serving plate; ladle mushroom mixture over toast. If desired, sprinkle with paprika; serve at once. Makes 4 servings.

A flavorful sandwich to serve as a main course for a luncheon party or light supper.

OPEN FACED HAM & CHICKEN SALAD SANDWICH

4 deli rye bread slices, cut from center of loaf

1/4 cup unsalted butter, room temperature

4 thin Black Forest or Westphalian ham slices

1 pint deli chicken salad

2 tablespoons mango chutney

1 small cucumber, peeled, thinly sliced

Lightly spread each bread slice with butter. Trim ham slices to just cover buttered bread. Chop leftover ham; place in a medium-size bowl. Stir in salad and chutney. Spoon mixture over ham-covered bread slices; top each sandwich with a row of cucumber slices. Makes 4 servings.

This round, flat loaf is truly unique—dense but not dry, the perfect pizza crust.

BOBOLI PIZZA

1 large round flat loaf boboli bread (see page 19)

1 large ripe tomato, cut into thick slices

About 1 tablespoon extra virgin olive oil

1 teaspoon mixed Italian herbs

6 or 8 pitted Niçoise olives, sliced

1/2 lb. fontina cheese, cut into thin slices

Preheat oven to 400F (205C). Line a baking sheet with foil. If frozen, let boboli bread stand at room temperature until thawed. Arrange tomato, slightly overlapping, over bread. Sprinkle with olive oil, herbs and olives. Overlap cheese over top slices. Place pizza on a foil-lined baking sheet. Bake in preheated oven only until cheese is partially melted and pizza is hot, about 8 to 10 minutes. Cut into wedges; serve at once. Makes 4 wedges.

Variations
Top boboli bread with chopped sun-dried tomatoes in olive oil, slivered calamata olives and provolone cheese slices. Bake and serve as directed above. Or top boboli with cottage cheese, chopped fresh strawberries, blueberries or sliced fresh peaches; sprinkle with powdered sugar. Bake as directed and serve as a breakfast or mid-morning treat.

This Sicilian specialty can be served hot or cold. Frozen dough makes it easy.

ITALIAN CALZONE

1 (1-lb.) loaf frozen bread dough, thawed

1/4 cup butter

2 or 3 dashes garlic juice

1/4 teaspoon mixed Italian herbs

1/2 lb. smoked turkey breast, cut in thin slices

1/2 lb. Black Forest or Westphalian ham, cut in thin slices

1/4 lb. provolone cheese, sliced

1/4 lb. mozzarella cheese, sliced

1/4 cup chopped, pitted Niçoise olives

Meatless spaghetti sauce, optional, heated

Preheat oven to 450F (230C). Roll dough to a 10" x 14" rectangle; cut off a 1/4-inch slice from 1 end and reserve. In a small bowl, combine butter, garlic juice and herbs. Spread 1/2 of mixture over dough. Top 1/2 of dough with layers of turkey, ham and cheese; sprinkle with olives. Fold uncovered side of dough over filling; press edges together to seal. Roll out reserved dough; cut into small stars or crescent shapes. Place on top of calzone and press lightly to hold them in place. Brush top and sides of calzone with remaining butter mixture. Bake in preheated oven about 20 minutes or until lightly browned. To serve, cut across into thick slices. Serve with spaghetti sauce, if desired. Makes 3 or 4 servings.

Serving suggestions: This hearty sandwich goes well with a rich red wine. Add a tossed green salad for a complete meal.

This sandwich was developed way back in the 1930s by Pat Olivieri for his sandwich restaurant stand in Philadelphia's Italian market. The stand is now a full-fledged restaurant, and they still serve this justly famous hero-style sandwich.

PAT'S ORIGINAL CHEESE STEAK SANDWICH

4 (6-inch-long) crusty Italian-style bread slices

6 tablespoons shredded Cheddar cheese

2 tablespoons corn oil or other vegetable oil

1 small green bell pepper, cut lengthwise into narrow strips

1 medium-size red onion, coarsely chopped

4 large mushrooms, coarsely chopped

3 tablespoons hot and spicy ketchup

3 to 4 dashes garlic juice

2 (1-inch-thick) beef fillet steaks, about 4 oz. each

Roasted bell peppers in oil

Dill pickle relish

Hot mustard

Cut each bread slice in half lengthwise, to but not through crust. Press each open and cover 1 side with shredded cheese. Set aside. Heat about 1 tablespoon of the oil in a large skillet over medium-high heat. Add bell pepper, onion and mushrooms. Cook, stirring constantly, about 2 minutes or until vegetables are crisp-tender. Transfer to a warm bowl; stir in ketchup and garlic juice. Preheat oven to 375F (190C). Cut steaks crosswise into 1/4-inch strips. Heat remaining oil in skillet over high heat. Add steak strips; cook until lightly browned. Stuff bread slices with steak strips and prepared vegetable mixture. Press sandwiches together; place on a baking sheet. Bake in preheated oven 2 to 3 minutes, or only until bread is warm and filling is reheated. Place each sandwich on a serving plate. Serve with roasted peppers, relish and mustard. Makes 4 sandwiches.

Inexpensive deviled ham transforms this sandwich into one that is devilishly good.

DEVILED HAM SANDWICHES

3 tablespoons butter, room temperature

1 (2-oz.) can deviled ham

1 tablespoon imported olive spread (olivata)

1 tablespoon Dijon-style mustard

Dash of hot pepper sauce

12 thin white bread slices

Combine butter, deviled ham, olive spread, mustard and hot pepper sauce in a medium-size bowl. Beat until well blended. Spread 6 slices of the bread with filling mixture, dividing evenly. Top each with a remaining bread slice. Cut off crusts, then cut each sandwich crosswise in 2 equal strips. If desired, stack and wrap sandwiches in foil or plastic wrap. Refrigerate up to 2 days or place in freezer up to 3 weeks. Bring to room temperature before serving. Makes 12 finger sandwiches.

When you taste this sandwich you might decide to become a vegetarian; it's that good!

DELUXE "VEGGY" SANDWICH

1/2 lb. ricotta cheese, drained

4 oz. mild, creamy chevre cheese

4 small radishes, chopped

1 small cucumber, peeled, seeded, coarsely chopped

Salt

1/2 teaspoon coarsely ground black pepper

1 to 2 dashes hot pepper sauce, optional

1 to 2 dashes garlic juice, optional

8 sourdough bread slices, cut from center of large loaf

3/4 to 1 cup packed bean sprouts

In a medium-size bowl, combine ricotta cheese and chevre; stir until blended. Stir in radishes and cucumber. Season with salt, pepper and, if desired, hot pepper sauce and garlic juice. Spread 1/2 of bread slices with cheese mixture. Top each with bean sprouts; cover each with remaining bread slice. Cut each sandwich diagonally in half. Makes 4 sandwiches.

Two different cheeses and especially delicious ham take this sandwich out of the ordinary.

GRILLED HAM & CHEESE SANDWICH DELUXE

For each sandwich:

2 thick firm white bread slices

1 thick fontina cheese slice

1 thin baked Virginia, Westphalian or Black Forest ham slice

1 firm ripe tomato slice

1 thick provolone cheese slice

2 tablespoons unsalted butter, room temperature

Cover 1 bread slice with fontina cheese slice; cover with ham slice and tomato slice. Top with provolone cheese slice and second slice of bread. Lightly press sandwich together, then spread 1/2 of the butter on outside of each bread slice. Heat a heavy skillet over medium heat. Add the sandwich; press down with back of a spatula; grill, turning once, until both sides are lightly browned. Serve at once. Serve hot. Makes 1 sandwich.

This is another Italian-American innovation. At its best, the hoagie includes not one but a variety of different cheeses and ham, plus shredded lettuce, sliced tomatoes and chopped onions. It's a meal of a sandwich.

ITALIAN-AMERICAN HOAGIE

4 large Italian-style crusty round or oblong rolls

About 1 tablespoon thick Italian-style salad dressing with garlic

Sprinkling of dried leaf oregano

Coarsely ground black pepper

4 thin slices of each of the following: capicolla ham, prosciutto, Genoa salami, mortadella and provolone cheese

About 1 cup loosely packed shredded Romaine or iceberg lettuce

4 thick tomato slices

4 paper-thin Vidalia or other mild onion slices

Cut each roll in half lengthwise. Spread cut side of each half with the dressing; sprinkle with oregano and pepper. Top bottom half of each roll with 1 slice of each meat and cheese, about 1/4 of the lettuce, 1 tomato slice and 1 onion slice. Cover with top half of roll; press down lightly to hold hoagie together. Makes 4 servings.

The "bread" for these sandwiches is made from commercially prepared puff pastry strips—a sandwich made in a gourmet's heaven.

GOURMET FRENCH HEROES

1 (7" x 5") strip all-butter frozen puff pastry (1/4 of 1-lb. pkg. frozen pastry)

2 tablespoons Dijon-style mustard

2 tablespoons mayonnaise

1/4 lb. thinly sliced imported Swiss cheese, cut in 5" x 3-1/2" strips

1/4 lb. thinly sliced baked Virginia ham, cut in 5" x 3-1/2" strips

6 thin fresh or frozen asparagus spears, cooked until crisp-tender

Pitted Niçoise olives

Preheat oven to 375F (190C). Cut pastry strip into 2 (5" x 3-1/2") strips. Place on a baking sheet. Bake in preheated oven until well puffed and lightly browned, about 20 minutes. Cool slightly. One at a time place a pastry strip on its side and cut lengthwise in half. With a small fork, scoop out and discard any soft, moist, unbaked pastry centers. In a small bowl, combine mustard and mayonnaise; stir until mixed. Spoon 1/2 of mixture on bottom half of each pastry strip. Cover each with 1/2 of the cheese and ham strips, then top with 3 cooked asparagus spears and spread with remaining mustard-mayonnaise mixture. Cover each with top pastry. With a spatula, transfer pastry sandwiches back to baking sheet and place in preheated oven 2 to 3 minutes, or until cheese is softened slightly. Place each sandwich on a small serving plate. If desired, spear an olive with a wooden pick and spear pick into top of each sandwich. Makes 2 sandwiches.

This positively sensational sandwich is great to take to a picnic or pot luck supper.

THE BIG BREAD SANDWICH

1 (1-lb.) round loaf sourdough or French bread

1 cup ricotta cheese, drained

1 tablespoon Parmesan cheese

1 tablespoon mayonnaise

1/4 cup minced fresh parsley, optional

1 teaspoon mixed dried Italian herbs

Salt and pepper

1 (6-oz.) jar Italian-style mushroom salad, drained

3/4 cup Italian-style vinaigrette dressing

1/4 lb. thinly sliced baked Virginia, Black Forest or Westphalian ham

1/4 lb. thinly sliced Swiss cheese

2 medium tomatoes, sliced

1/4 lb. thinly sliced Genoa salami

Place bread on its side; cut it in 4 equal (about 1-inch thick) slices. In a medium-size bowl, combine ricotta cheese, Parmesan cheese, mayonnaise and, if desired, parsley. Stir in Italian herbs, salt and pepper. Spread about 3/4 of cheese mixture on bottom layer of bread. Cover with about 1/2 of the mushroom salad. Top with second slice of bread. Spread this slice with about 1/3 of the dressing. Cover with ham and cheese slices. Cover with third slice of bread. Spread with remaining cheese mixture, top with tomato slices, salami and remaining mushroom salad. Spread the remaining salad dressing over the cut side of the top layer, then place cut side down on sandwich. Serve immediately or wrap the entire sandwich in plastic wrap. Place on a large plate; cover with an inverted pie pan, then top pie pan with something heavy, like a small heavy skillet, to weigh the sandwich down. Refrigerator up to 24 hours. To serve, place on a large cutting board. Cut loaf from top to bottom into 5 or 6 thick slices, then cut each slice in half. Makes 8 to 12 servings.

SALADS

If eaten each day any one of the recipes to follow can, like the proverbial apple, help keep the doctor away. Each contains a goodly amount of crisp, crunchy fresh lettuce or other fresh vegetables. But you don't have to eat them just for the sake of their healthful qualities but also because they are full of satisfying flavors and textures.

Some words about salads in general: Because most salads taste best at room temperature, do not, as many cookbooks still advise, "chill before serving." Though all salads are simple and quick to prepare, there are several necessary steps to making a truly superb one. First, lettuce leaves or other greenery must be washed, then thoroughly dried before using or the dressing, when added, will not flavor and coat the leaves, but fall to the bottom of the bowl. Add tomatoes to salads only if they have been seeded, cut into strips and blotted thoroughly dry. As their juices will "water down" the dressing, add tomato slices or wedges around the edge of the salad bowl as a garnish. When adding a dressing to a salad, add it a little at a time, using only enough to moisten the salad. Serve any remaining dressing separately. You can vary vegetables or other ingredients in any salad, using what's in season or what you have on hand. No salad need take more than a short time to prepare, but you will be rewarded with true appreciation and praise if you take the time to garnish them nicely and arrange them neatly, with an eye to their visual appeal. Use pretty salad plates, lettuce-lined clear glass salad bowls or individual bowls.

You can serve any of the salads as a first course, with the first course, as a separate course after the main course, or as the main course itself.

A hearty salad to add to a multi-dish supper party menu, it goes beautifully with baked ham.

WHITE BEAN & WALNUT SALAD

1 (16-oz.) can white kidney beans

2 (1/2-oz.) pkgs. (about 1/2 cup) chopped walnuts

1 cup loosely packed bean sprouts, or 1 cup shredded Romaine lettuce

1/4 cup minced chives

1/4 to 1/3 cup vinaigrette dressing or poppy seed dressing

Crisp lettuce leaves, optional

Place beans in a colander; rinse under cold water until water runs clears. Blot dry with paper towels, then transfer to a large bowl. Add walnuts, bean sprouts and chives. Add dressing; toss to mix. Refrigerate until ready to serve. If desired, line a serving bowl or plates with lettuce. Spoon salad into serving bowl or spoon onto salad plates. Serves 4 as a main course, 6 to 8 as part of a multi-dish buffet supper.

Definitely a salad for those who refuse to take salad making seriously, but who want to make a lasting impression.

GRAPEFRUIT & AVOCADO SALAD WITH SEAFOOD

1/2 to 3/4 lb. fresh or frozen thawed lobster, crabmeat or imitation crabmeat

1/4 cup clear French dressing

1 tablespoon chili sauce

1 (1-pint) jar grapefruit sections

1 medium-size avocado, cut in bite-size cubes

Crisp romaine lettuce leaves

Place seafood in a large bowl; stir in French dressing and chili sauce. Cover and refrigerate 30 minutes. Stir in grapefruit sections and avocado cubes. Serve over lettuce. Makes 4 main course servings.

This main course salad in a wonderfully complex mix of textures and tastes.

WALDORF AVOCADO SALAD

2 medium-size avocados, halved, pitted

1 tablespoon lemon or lime juice

1/2 lb. cooked, peeled shrimp or 1 (5- or 6-oz.) pkg. frozen, cooked, peeled, shrimp, thawed

1 oz. chopped walnuts

1 small tart apple, cored, peeled, finely chopped

3 oz. walnut gourmandise cheese, chopped

2 tablespoons mayonnaise

1 teaspoon lemon or lime juice, optional

Crisp lettuce leaves

Rub each avocado with 1 tablespoon lemon or lime juice. In a large bowl, combine shrimp, walnuts, apple and cheese. Stir in mayonnaise and, if desired, 1 teaspoon lemon or lime juice. Line 4 plates with lettuce. Place avocado halves on lettuce-lined plates; top with filling mixture, letting excess fall onto lettuce. Makes 4 servings.

We like to serve this spectacular salad either before or after the main course.

PEAR SALAD WITH BLUE CHEESE FILLING

2 large ripe pears, peeled, halved, cored

1 tablespoon lemon juice

1 (3-oz.) pkg. cream cheese, room temperature

2 oz. blue cheese, room temperature

1 teaspoon lemon juice

1 tablespoon Dijon-style mustard

1 (2-oz.) pkg. chopped walnuts

Crisp lettuce leaves

Brush pears on all sides with 1 tablespoon lemon juice; set aside. In a medium-size bowl, combine cream cheese, blue cheese, 1 teaspoon lemon juice and mustard. Blend until smooth; stir in walnuts. Fill each pear half with mixture, mounding it high. Refrigerate until ready to serve. Arrange lettuce leaves on 4 individual salad plates; place pear halves on lettuce. Makes 4 servings.

*he guacamole for this salad requires only five in-
redients, nonetheless, it's the best we ever ate.*

GUACAMOLE SALAD

large or 2 medium-size ripe avocados

tablespoon lemon juice

tablespoons concentrated Bloody Mary mix

or 2 small green onions, minced

or 2 medium-size radishes, finely chopped

risp lettuce leaves

thick tomato slices

tablespoon clear French dressing

itted and sliced ripe olives, optional

ut avocado in half; remove and reserve pit. Scoop
lp from shell into a medium-size bowl; mash with a
rk until smooth. Stir in lemon juice, Bloody Mary
ix, green onion and radishes. Place avocado pit in
enter of bowl; cover and refrigerate until ready to
rve. (Avocado pit will keep guacamole from dis-
oloring.) To serve, cover 4 small salad plates with
ttuce leaves; top each with a tomato slice. Discard
t from guacamole; spoon guacamole over tomato
ices. Drizzle with dressing. Garnish, if desired,
ith olives. Makes 4 servings.

ariation
his guacamole can also be served as a dip or filling
r tortillas.

---

*This is both a colorful and delicious salad that will
take you only about 10 minutes to prepare. Bonus: it
can be prepared ahead and stored in the refrigerator
until ready to serve.*

CAULIFLOWER & BROCCOLI SALAD WITH SOUR CREAM DRESSING

1/2 lb. broccoli flowerets from salad bar

1/2 lb. cauliflowerets from salad bar

1/2 to 1 (8-oz.) carton dairy sour cream

2 tablespoons white wine vinegar

1/4 cup (1 oz.) shredded Cheddar cheese

1 teaspoon Dijon-style or Dusseldorf mustard

2 to 4 tablespoons fresh or frozen minced
chives, thawed

8 to 10 ripe olives, pitted, sliced

Salt and coarsely ground black pepper

1 large tomato, seeded, chopped

Place broccoli and cauliflower flowerets on a steamer rack over simmering water. Cover; steam about 3
minutes or until crisp-tender. Transfer to a large
bowl; set aside. In a medium-size bowl, combine
remaining ingredients. Add to steamed vegetables;
toss to mix thoroughly. Serve at room temperature
or cover and refrigerate until about 15 minutes before serving. Makes 6 to 8 servings.

The frozen vegetables used in this salad are crisp, delicious and nutritious because they are briefly blanched, not cooked.

VEGETABLE SALAD, EMERGENCY SHELF STYLE

1 (10-oz.) pkg. frozen chopped mixed vegetables

1 (16-oz.) can Italian-style whole tomatoes, drained, chopped, or 1 large tomato, halved, seeded, cut in narrow strips

2 or 3 crisp sweet pickles, chopped

1 tablespoon juice from pickles

2 tablespoons Italian-style vinaigrette dressing or other bottled dressing of your choice

Optional additions: minced fresh or frozen chives, 1 or 2 celery stalks, thinly sliced

Place frozen block of vegetables in a colander; rinse under cold water until separated. Transfer to a large bowl; cover by about 1 inch with boiling water. Let stand about 2 minutes, stirring occasionally. Drain and place in a salad bowl. Add tomatoes, pickles, pickle juice and dressing. Toss to mix. If desired, stir in chives and/or celery; toss lightly. Serve at room temperature or cover and refrigerate until ready to serve. Makes 4 servings.

We think our version of this well-beloved American salad classic is even better than the original.

CAESAR SALAD

1 head Romaine lettuce, thinly sliced crosswise

1 egg yolk

2 tablespoons mayonnaise

2 tablespoons lemon juice

1 or 2 dashes garlic juice

1 (2-oz.) can anchovy fillets

1/2 cup grated Parmesan cheese

1 cup garlic-flavored croutons

Black pepper

2 hard-cooked eggs, quartered

Place lettuce in a large salad bowl. In a small bowl, combine egg yolk, mayonnaise, lemon juice and garlic juice. Drain and chop anchovies, reserving oil. Stir chopped anchovies and reserved oil into mayonnaise mixture. Add to lettuce in bowl; toss thoroughly. Add cheese, croutons and pepper. Toss again before serving. Garnish with hard-cooked eggs. Makes 4 servings.

This Italian classic looks and tastes divine; a wonderful platter to add to your buffet table.

TURKEY TONNATO PLATTER

2 (3-1/2-oz.) cans tuna packed in olive oil, drained

1 (8.6-oz.) jar bernaise sauce

2 tablespoons lemon juice

1 tablespoon Dijon-style mustard

2 or 3 dashes hot pepper sauce

1 pint deli potato salad

2 tablespoons fresh or frozen minced chives

24 thin slices cooked turkey breast, about 2 lbs.

Crisp lettuce leaves

2 tablespoons capers, drained

Small ripe cherry tomatoes

Place 1 can of the tuna and about 3/4 of the bernaise sauce in work bowl of food processor or blender; process until smooth. Transfer mixture to a medium-size bowl; stir in lemon juice, mustard and hot pepper sauce. Place second can of tuna in another bowl; break up with a fork. Add potato salad, chives and bernaise sauce mixture; stir gently to mix. One at a time, place a small amount of the tuna-potato salad mixture on a turkey slice and roll up. Line a large oblong platter with lettuce. Arrange stuffed turkey rolls in a single layer on lettuce. Spoon remaining bernaise sauce across center of rolls and sprinkle capers over sauce. Garnish platter with cherry tomatoes. Makes 6 to 8 servings.

For a complete menu, you might serve this salad with egg rolls and batter fried shrimp from your favorite Chinese restaurant.

ORIENTAL-STYLE TURKEY SALAD

3 tablespoons tahine paste

2 or 3 dashes garlic juice

2 tablespoons rice vinegar or white wine vinegar

1 tablespoon soy sauce

1/2 teaspoon dried red pepper flakes

1/4 cup chicken broth or water

Salt

1 (8-oz.) pkg. frozen Chinese pea pods

1 small cucumber, peeled, seeded, chopped

1 small red bell pepper, cut in thin slivers

1/2 lb. smoked turkey from deli, thinly sliced, cut in narrow strips

Crisp lettuce leaves

2 green onions, sliced diagonally

1 (2-1/2-oz.) pkg. slivered almonds

In a large bowl, combine tahine paste, garlic juice, vinegar, soy sauce, pepper flakes and broth. Season to taste with salt. Stir to blend; set aside. Bring a large pot of water to a boil; add pea pods and return water to full boil. Drain pea pods into a colander; add to tahine mixture. Add cucumber, bell pepper and turkey; toss gently to mix ingredients. Arrange lettuce leaves on 4 salad plates. Spoon over crisp lettuce leaves; scatter green onions and almonds over top of salads. Makes 4 servings.

Consider the assets: this salad never fails to please just about everyone. It's quick and easy to prepare, can be made ahead and is a colorful addition to a buffet party supper table.

SALAD NIÇOISE FOR A CROWD

2 lbs. small new potatoes	**18 to 20 pitted Niçoise or other ripe olives**
2 pints deli three-bean salad, drained	**2 tablespoons lemon juice**
3 celery stalks, diagonally cut in thin slices	**About 1/2 cup creamy Italian-style salad dressing**
1/2 lb. ripe plum tomatoes, quartered	**Lettuce leaves to line salad bowl**
1 small bunch green onions, thinly sliced	
2 (7-1/2- or 8-oz.) cans tuna packed in water or olive oil, drained	**3 or 4 hard-cooked eggs, sliced**
	Ripe olives

Scrub potatoes, then place them in a large pot of rapidly boiling water. Cover and cook 10 to 12 minutes or until tender when pierced with a small knife. Drain and rinse under cold running water. Pat dry; let stand until cooled to room temperature, cut in half or quarters. Place in a large bowl; add three-bean salad, celery, tomatoes and onions. Top with tuna, using a fork to gently break tuna into small chunks. Add Niçoise olives, lemon juice and salad dressing; toss with 2 forks to mix ingredients thoroughly. Cover and refrigerate until about 1/2 hour before serving. Line a large bowl with lettuce. Spoon salad into lettuce-lined bowl. Arrange eggs around edge of bowl and top with olives. Serves 8 to 12 as part of a buffet supper.

Variation
Line a large platter with lettuce leaves. Arrange individual ingredients on lettuce. Serve dressing separately.

Serving suggestions: This salad can be part of a buffet or served alone with crunchy dinner rolls and iced tea.

This salad features a new way to "cook" frozen vegetables so that they are crisp-tender.

PASTA SALAD, CALIFORNIA STYLE

1 (10-oz.) pkg. frozen tiny green peas

1 teaspoon vegetable oil

1/2 teaspoon salt

1 (8-oz.) pkg. rotelli, cavatelli or other pasta

1/2 cup Italian-style vinaigrette dressing

8 to 12 cherry tomatoes, halved, seeded

1 small avocado, chopped

Chopped pistachios or almonds, optional

Place frozen peas in a large bowl; cover with boiling water. Let stand about 1 minute, then drain into a colander. Set aside in colander. Bring a large pot of water to a full boil; add oil and salt. Add pasta; cook, stirring occasionally, until tender yet firm to the bite. Drain over peas in colander. Transfer to a large bowl; add dressing, tomatoes and avocado. Toss to mix. If desired, sprinkle salad with chopped nuts. Serve at room temperature. Makes 6 to 8 servings.

Imitation crabmeat is a combination of white fish and crabmeat. It can be found in the fresh seafood department at your supermarket.

ORIENTAL SEAFOOD SALAD

3 tablespoons lime juice

1 tablespoon soy sauce

2 tablespoons light and fruity olive oil or vegetable oil

1/4 teaspoon crushed red pepper flakes

Salt

1 lb. imitation crabmeat, thawed, if frozen

4 to 5 oz. Chinese vermicelli, broken into short strands

1 medium-size cucumber, peeled, seeded, thinly sliced

6 to 8 radishes, thinly sliced

In a large bowl, combine lime juice, soy sauce and oil. Beat with a fork until well blended. Stir in crushed pepper flakes and salt. Add crabmeat; toss to mix. Cover and store in refrigerator until ready to use. (The mixture may be made up to 3 hours ahead.) Place vermicelli in a large bowl; cover by about 1 inch with boiling water. Let stand about 15 minutes or until tender. Drain, rinse under cold water and drain thoroughly. Add noodles, cucumber and radishes to crabmeat; toss to mix. Spoon onto 4 salad plates. Makes 4 servings.

You'll find both the chicken and the ham at your deli and these days you'll find fresh pineapple already peeled and cored in the produce department of your supermarket.

HOT CHICKEN SALAD WITH MANGO CHUTNEY & HAM

1/2 cup half and half

1 teaspoon curry powder

1 tablespoon Major Grey's mango chutney, diced

1 pint deli chicken salad

4 firm white bread slices, toasted

4 thick baked Virginia ham slices, about 1/2 lb. total weight

Paprika

4 thick fresh pineapple slices, cut in cubes, or 1 (8-oz.) can pineapple cubes in natural juice, drained, optional

Small clusters of seedless green grapes, optional

Preheat oven to 350F (175C). Line a baking sheet with foil. Pour half and half into the top half of a double boiler over simmering water; stir in curry powder. Add mango chutney and chicken salad. Cook, stirring, about 5 minutes or until mixture is hot. Cover and keep hot over simmering water. Place toast on 4 serving plates. Place ham on foil-lined baking sheet. Bake in preheated oven until hot. Place a ham slice on each bread slice; cover with hot chicken mixture, dividing evenly. Sprinkle with paprika and, if desired, garnish with pineapples cubes and grape clusters. Makes 4 servings.

This home-prepared version takes no more time to prepare than it would take you to drive to that Mexican restaurant. In addition, the flavor is more "ole."

TACO SALAD

1 tablespoon avocado oil or vegetable oil

3/4 lb. lean ground beef

1/2 cup mild or hot salsa or taco sauce

1/2 cup drained, canned red kidney beans

1 small Vidalia or red onion, chopped or 2 oz. chopped onion from supermarket salad bar

1/2 small green bell pepper, chopped or about 2-1/2 oz. chopped green bell pepper from supermarket salad bar

Salt and black pepper

2 cups shredded Romaine or iceberg lettuce

1 (7-1/2-oz.) pkg. taco chips

3/4 cup (about 3-oz.) shredded Monterey Jack or Mild cheddar cheese

Tomato wedges

Calamata olives

Heat oil in a large heavy skillet over medium-high heat. Add meat; cook, stirring, until no longer pink, about 1 minute. Stir in salsa, beans, onion and bell pepper. Season with salt and pepper; cook about 2 minutes more. Place lettuce on 4 salad serving plates. Top with meat mixture; sprinkle with cheese. Surround with 1/2 of taco chips; garnish with tomato wedges and olives. Serve remaining taco chips separately. Makes 4 or 6 servings.

A festive salad for a main course luncheon entree. Especially delicious when served with thin wedges of heated boboli bread and a chilled glass of light white wine.

SALMON SALAD WITH BROCCOLI, OLIVES & CHERRY TOMATOES

1/2 lb. broccoli flowerets	**Salt and pepper**
1 (15-1/2-oz.) can red sockeye salmon, drained, flaked	**Crisp lettuce leaves**
	Sicilian green olives and Greek ripe olives
Sour Cream Dressing, page 140	**Hard-cooked eggs, quartered**
2 tablespoons lemon juice	**Cherry tomatoes**
1 lb. small new potatoes, cooked	

Place broccoli in boiling water in a medium-sized saucepan. Cook, uncovered, 2 to 3 minutes or until crisp-tender. Drain; set aside. Make dressing; set aside. Place salmon in a large bowl. Sprinkle with lemon juice; toss lightly. Peel and cut potatoes into wedges; add to salmon. Add broccoli and dressing; toss lightly to mix. Season with salt and pepper. Line 4 serving plates with lettuce leaves. Top each with salad. Garnish with olives, eggs and tomatoes. Makes 4 servings.

Variation
Substitute cauliflowerets for potatoes. Cook with broccoli. Continue as above.

Serving suggestions: Perfect for a summer luncheon. Serve with heated boboli bread. Mississippi Mud Parfaits, page 146, would make a perfect ending.

Rich tasing, yet it's quick and easy!

SOUR CREAM DRESSING

1/2 cup dairy sour cream

1/4 cup mayonnaise

1 teaspoon Dijon-style or other hot mustard

1 tablespoon minced chives

Salt and pepper

Place all ingredients in a small bowl; beat with a fork until blended. Makes about 3/4 cup.

This hearty salad makes great picnic fare. We prefer to make it with genuine Swiss Emmentaler but almost any other cheese firm enough to cut into julienne strips can be used.

SWISS CHEESE & HAM SALAD

1 lb. Emmentaler or similar cheese, thinly sliced, cut into long matchstick strips

1/2 lb. baked Virginia ham, Black Forest ham or Westphalian ham, thinly sliced, cut into long matchstick strips

6 to 8 tablespoons mustard-flavored vinaigrette dressing

2 to 3 cups shredded Romaine lettuce

Combine cheese, ham and dressing in a large bowl. Let stand at room temperature about 30 minutes or cover and refrigerate for several hours. Just before serving, add lettuce; toss to combine. Makes 4 to 6 servings.

Made from soaked bulghur wheat, tabouleh is a popular Mid-Eastern salad that can also be served as an appetizer. Our version, made with deli carrot salad is crisp, crunchy and delicious.

TABOULEH WITH CARROT SALAD & POPPY SEED DRESSING

1 cup bulghur wheat

1/2 pint deli carrot salad with raisins, drained

2 tablespoons chopped crystallized ginger

1/4 cup thick and creamy poppy seed dressing

1/4 teaspoon dried hot red pepper flakes

1/4 teaspoon ground cumin, optional

Crisp lettuce leaves

Small clusters of green grapes

Place bulghur in a large bowl; cover by about 1 inch with boiling water. Let stand until almost all water has been absorbed, about 20 minutes. With your hands, press out any remaining water. Stir in carrot salad and chopped ginger. Add remaining ingredients except lettuce; toss to mix. If desired, refrigerate salad until about 1/2 hour before using. When ready to serve, line a bowl with lettuce; spoon in salad. Garnish with grape clusters. Makes 6 to 8 servings.

Variation
Use a thoroughly drained "health" salad from your deli instead of carrot salad or use well-drained cole slaw.

An excellent choice for a main course luncheon party dish.

SEAFOOD SALAD WITH LOUIS DRESSING

Louis Dressing, see below

Crisp lettuce leaves

3/4 to 1 lb. lump crabmeat (thawed if frozen), imitation crabmeat, or peeled, deveined cooked shrimp (or a combination)

12 thick tomato slices

4 marinated artichoke hearts, drained, halved

4 hard-cooked eggs, halved

Pitted Niçoise olives

Lemon wedges

LOUIS DRESSING

3/4 cup mayonnaise

1/4 cup chili sauce

2 teaspoons lemon juice

2 teaspoons prepared horseradish

1 tablespoon minced fresh or frozen chives

1 or 2 dashes hot pepper sauce

Salt and pepper

Prepare dressing; refrigerate until chilled. Line 4 luncheon plates with lettuce leaves. Arrange seafood on 1 side of each plate. Place 3 tomato slices slightly overlapping on other side of each plate. Garnish each plate with artichoke hearts and hard-cooked eggs halves. Spoon some of the Louis Dressing over each seafood serving. Garnish each plate with olives and lemon wedges. Serve remain-ing dressing separately. If desired, refrigerate salads until ready to serve. Makes 4 servings.

LOUIS DRESSING
In a medium-size bowl, combine ingredients; blend well. Makes 1 cup dressing.

You could spend hours preparing a salad and not come up with a better one.

WHITE BEAN & TUNA SALAD

1 (1-lb.) can cannelini (white kidney beans) beans

6 or 8 chopped pitted ripe olives

1/4 cup mild light and fruity olive oil or avocado oil

2 tablespoons white wine vinegar

Salt and pepper

1 (8-oz. can) solid pack tuna, drained

2 tablespoons olive or avocado oil

About 2 tablespoons minced parsley or fresh or frozen minced chives

Drain beans into a colander and rinse under cold running water until water runs clear. Transfer to a large bowl; stir in olives, the 1/4 cup oil and vinegar. Season lightly with salt and pepper; toss to mix. Break tuna into chunks and place on top of beans. Pour remaining oil over top; sprinkle with parsley or chives. Makes 4 or 6 servings.

Ziti and cheese have always been an American favorite yet they appear new when served as a salad.

PASTA & CHEESE SALAD

1/2 cup dairy sour cream

1/2 cup buttermilk

1/2 cup minced fresh or frozen chives

2 tablespoons Dijon-style mustard

1/2 teaspoon salt

1/4 teaspoon pepper

1 teaspoon vegetable oil

1/2 teaspoon salt

1 (8-oz.) pkg. ziti or other small pasta shapes

1/2 lb. smoked ham, cut in strips

6 oz. Swiss cheese, cut in narrow strips

Minced parsley, optional

In a large bowl, combine sour cream, buttermilk, chives, mustard, salt and pepper. Beat with a fork until well blended. Bring a large pot of water to a full boil. Stir in oil and salt. Add pasta; cook, stirring occasionally, until tender yet firm to the bite. Drain into a colander, then add to bowl of dressing mixture. Add ham and cheese; toss to mix. Serve at room temperature or refrigerate until about 1/2 hour before serving. If desired, garnish with minced parsley. Makes 6 to 8 servings.

This salad was developed for occasions when you don't have time to shop for fresh ingredients.

PASTA SALAD WITH TURKEY PROVENÇAL

1 (6-oz.) jar marinated artichoke hearts

1 (1-lb.) can Italian imported whole tomatoes with basil

2 or 3 dashes garlic juice

1 tablespoon mild fruity olive oil

1 tablespoon tarragon vinegar

1/2 teaspoon sugar

6 or 8 pitted Niçoise olives, sliced

1/4 lb. smoked turkey breast, cut in narrow strips

1 teaspoon vegetable oil

1/2 teaspoon salt

1 (8-oz.) pkg. small elbow macaroni

1 tablespoon fresh or frozen minced chives

Drain oil from artichokes into a large skillet; add 1/4 cup juice from canned tomatoes, stir in garlic juice, olive oil and vinegar. Add sugar. Bring to a boil, stirring, over high heat. Reduce heat; simmer 2 to 3 minutes. Transfer to a large bowl. Add drained artichoke hearts. Drain and discard remaining juice from tomatoes; add tomatoes to bowl. Using a small knife, break up artichoke hearts and tomatoes. Add olives and turkey strips; set aside. Bring a large pot of water to a full boil; stir in vegetable oil and salt. Add macaroni; cook, stirring occasionally, until macaroni is tender yet firm to the bite. Drain into a colander; add to bowl with tomatoes and artichokes. Toss salad to mix well; sprinkle with minced chives. Serve at room temperature. Makes 4 servings.

DOUBLE-QUICK DESSERTS

The more things change, the more they remain the same, or so the saying goes. But it's true—though Mom may still make the "very best apple pie you ever ate," more likely than not, if she really deserves that reputation, she now owns her very own bakery where you can buy it fresh from her oven. Back home, you can serve it as she did, warm and topped with wonderfully flavorful commercially prepared ice cream; the kind it once took hours to make.

These days you can find all of the component parts for a truly great dessert easy to buy, take home and transform into your very own, homemade creation. What's more, they're even better than you remembered them. They're lighter, less filling than those of our American past, yet, that is not to say they are always low in calories. Far from it, they are, for the most part, wickedly rich and totally satisfying. You won't find your sweet tooth short-changed; the only short thing about these desserts is the short time you will need to triumphantly bring them to the table. Enjoy them without guilt—you deserve it.

You'll need only three ingredients to make these fabulously rich and impressive little tarts.

CHOCOLATE-PECAN TARTS

6 (2-3/4" x 1") ready-to-fill chocolate dessert shells

6 tablespoons canned pecan filling for cakes, pastries and desserts

6 small scoops butter pecan ice cream

Pecan halves, optional

Fill each chocolate shell with 1 tablespoon of the pecan filling. Top with a scoop of butter pecan ice cream and, if desired, garnish each tart with a pecan half. Makes 6 tarts.

Variations
Chocolate Nesselrode Tarts
Fill each chocolate shell with about 1 tablespoon prepared Nesselrode sauce; top each with a small scoop of vanilla ice cream. If desired, garnish each with a dollop of the Nesselrode sauce.
Chocolate Melba Tarts
Fill each chocolate shell with about 1 tablespoon prepared melba sauce; top each with a small scoop of raspberry sherbert. If desired, garnish each with a dollop of the melba sauce.
Chocolate Apricot Tarts
Fill each chocolate shell with about 1 tablespoon apricot jam; top each with a small scoop of vanilla ice cream. Place a drained canned apricot half, cut side down, over ice cream.

Despite the title, this Mexican-style dessert can be served any night of the week.

MEXICAN SATURDAY NIGHT SUNDAE

4 large or 8 small scoops coffee ice cream

1/4 teaspoon ground cinnamon

1/4 cup coffee-flavored liqueur

1/2 cup chocolate fudge topping

1/4 cup double or triple creme cheese or lightly whipped cream, optional

Instant expresso coffee powder, optional

Place 1 large or 2 small scoops of ice cream in each of 4 parfait glasses or dessert bowls. If desired, let ice cream soften in refrigerator while you enjoy the main course of your meal. When ready to serve, sprinkle each serving lightly with cinnamon and top with 1 tablespoon of the liqueur. Spoon chocolate topping over each serving and, if desired, garnish each with cheese or whipped cream and sprinkle lightly with coffee powder. Makes 4 servings.

This after dinner classic drink is a colorful combination of liqueurs layered, one over the other, in a small stemmed glass. Our version, made with ice cream, creates the same rainbow of colors and is even more delicious yet much less alcoholic. For this creation you will need tall, narrow stemmed cordial or wine glasses or parfait glasses. Use a melon baller or small ice cream scoop for balls. If making ice cream balls ahead, freeze on a baking sheet.

ICE CREAM POUSSE-CAFE

1 tablespoon green creme de menthe

4 small scoops vanilla ice cream

3 small scoops strawberry ice cream

1 tablespoon commercially prepared strawberry ice cream topping

1 tablespoon kirsch

3 small scoops chocolate ice cream

1 tablespoon coffee-flavored liqueur

Any one of the following: green or red maraschino cherry, chopped walnuts or pecans, grated dark chocolate candy or sprinkling of instant expresso powder

Pour creme de menthe into bottom of a stemmed glass; top with 3 scoops of the vanilla ice cream. Top with strawberry ice cream balls, strawberry topping and kirsch. Add chocolate ice cream balls to glass; pour coffee liqueur over them. Top with remaining scoop of vanilla ice cream, garnish as desired. Serve at once. Makes 1 serving.

Variation
Any number of different flavors and colors of both ice cream and liqueurs can be used to assemble this dessert creation.

A dessert for Christmas or New Year's Eve, or at any other festive occasion. I serve it in brandy snifters or stemmed wine glasses.

HOLIDAY SIN

1/4 cup prepared Nesselrode sauce

4 large scoops vanilla ice cream

1/2 cup frozen unsweetened grated coconut, thawed

1/2 cup Cointreau or other orange-flavored liqueur

Red or green maraschino cherries, optional

For each serving, spoon 1 tablespoon Nesselrode sauce into bottom of a brandy snifter or wine glass; top with a scoop of ice cream and sprinkle with coconut. Place in freezer until about 15 minutes before serving, if desired. To finish, pour in Cointreau, and if desired, garnish with a cherry. Serve at once. Makes 4 servings.

You don't have to be from Mississippi to thoroughly enjoy this truly superb dessert.

MISSISSIPPI MUD PARFAIT

1/2 cup honey

1/4 cup bourbon whiskey

4 large or 8 small scoops chocolate ice cream

About 2 tablespoons toasted slivered almonds

1/4 cup dairy sour cream, optional

Place jar of honey in a small pan of very hot water until warmed. Measure and pour into a medium-size bowl. Stir in bourbon. Place 1 large scoop of the chocolate ice cream in each of 4 dessert dishes. Pour bourbon-honey mixture over each. Sprinkle each serving with almonds; if desired, top each with a dollop of sour cream. Makes 4 servings.

Serving Suggestions: Serve this as the final touch to a light meal, or serve as part of an ice cream sundae party. Choose a variety of cookies, ice cream flavors and other toppings.

You will need an electric skillet, fondue pot or chafing dish that you can bring to the table to prepare this dramatic dessert. Nonetheless, it's easy to prepare and your guests will not only love it, but be impressed with your expertise. Just bring everything to the table before you begin.

FRUITE FLAMBÉ

1/2 cup brandy

1 (1-lb.) can pitted dark sweet cherries

1 (1-lb.) can apricot halves

1 (1-lb.) can pineapple chunks

6 sugar cubes

2 teaspoons lemon extract

Vanilla ice cream or poundcake slices, or both

Heat brandy in a small saucepan over medium heat until hot. Transfer to a small pitcher. Drain all fruit, combining syrups; reserve 1 cup syrup. Combine and place fruit in chafing dish over simmering water, electric skillet or fondue pot. Arrange ice cream or pound cake in serving dishes. Bring to serving table; add the 1 cup reserved syrup to fruit. Heat until liquid simmers, 6 to 8 minutes. Place sugar cubes in a small dish; sprinkle with lemon extract. Place cubes on top of hot fruit, carefully pour in brandy and ignite. If desired, dim electric lights for a more dramatic effect. When flame dies, ladle fruit and liquid over ice cream or poundcake. Makes 6 to 8 servings.

A festive yet simple way to prepare dessert that makes use of one of summer's most delectable fruits.

PLUMS WITH TRIPLE CREME

1/4 lb. Saint Andre or other triple creme cheese

2 tablespoons cognac or other top-quality brandy

4 large ripe plums, halved, pitted

3 tablespoons light or dark brown sugar

Cover a baking sheet with foil. Preheat broiler. In a small bowl, combine cheese and brandy; beat with a fork until smooth and fluffy. Set aside. Arrange plum halves, cut side up, on foil-covered baking sheet. Fill center of each with brown sugar, mounding it slightly. Broil about 2 inches from heat 4 to 5 minutes or until sugar begins to bubble and brown. Let stand at room temperature to cool slightly. Just before serving, top each plum with cheese mixture. Makes 4 servings.

A typically Italian-style creation.

PEACHES STUFFED WITH AMARETTO FILLING

4 large firm ripe peaches

4 amaretto cookies

1/4 cup mirabelle (plum brandy), Galiano liqueur or kirsch

Lightly sweetened whipped cream or ricotta cheese

Dip each peach in boiling water for a few seconds; peel. Cut in half, remove pit. Place peach halves, cut side down, on steamer rack over simmering water. Cover and steam until peaches are just tender, 4 to 6 minutes. Place 4 of the peach halves, cut side up, on 4 small rimmed dessert plates. Place 1 amaretto cookie on each and sprinkle with about 1 teaspoon of the liqueur. Cover with a peach half, press down; place plates in refrigerator until peaches are chilled, or until ready to serve. Spoon remaining liqueur over peaches, then spoon whipped cream around each. Makes 4 servings.

We like to serve this light yet rich dessert with crisp rolled cookies; Pepperidge Farm makes some of the best.

BRANDIED PEACHES WITH APRICOT CREAM

1/2 cup whipping cream

1/2 cup creamy-style apricot yogurt

1 egg white

2 tablespoons superfine sugar

1 (16-oz.) jar brandied peach halves

Rolled cookies

In a medium-size bowl, whip the cream until stiff peaks form. Fold in the yogurt. In a separate bowl, beat the egg white until soft peaks form. Gradually beat in sugar to make a stiff meringue; fold into cream and yogurt mixture. Drain peach halves (reserve syrup for other use) and arrange them, cut side down, on 1 side of 4 small dessert plates. Spoon some of the apricot cream on other side of each plate. Arrange 2 or 3 rolled cookies on each serving. Serve at once. Makes 4 servings.

Not a true English trifle but just as festive and equally pretty. Buy the merinque shells from a top-notch bakery or the bakery department of your supermarket. Use only the freshest and most perfect berries. Prepare the berries ahead but don't put this together until just before serving.

SUMMERTIME TRIFLE

1 pint strawberries, hulled

6 or 8 large meringue shells or about twice that many miniature meringues

1/2 cup whipping cream

4 tablespoons superfine sugar, or granulated sugar put through a sieve or whirled in a food processor a few seconds

2 tablespoons Kirsch or a orange-flavored liqueur

Reserve 6 large perfect berries for garnish. Coarsely chop remaining berries; place in a medium-size bowl. Add whole berries, cover bowl and refrigerate until chilled or until ready to use, but no more than 3 or 4 hours. With your hands, crumble each meringue over a medium-size bowl. Set aside at room temperature until ready to use. In another medium-size bowl, beat cream until thick. Add 2 tablespoons sugar a little at a time and continue to beat until stiff. Just before serving, place about half of the crumbled meringue shells in the bottom of 6 stemmed wine or parfait glasses. Cover each with about half of the chopped berries and sprinkle lightly with the remaining sugar and Kirsch. Repeat with another layer of meringue shells, then berries and top with whipped cream. Garnish each serving with a whole berry. Makes 6 servings.

Serving suggestions: This pretty dessert and pink champagne would be the perfect ending to a hearty main dish.